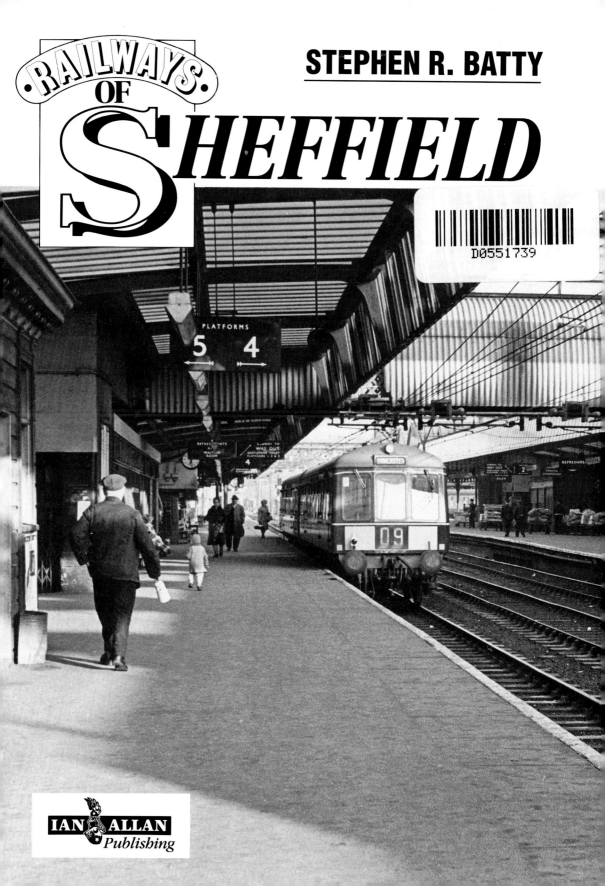

# RAILWAYS OF SHEFFIELD

## STEPHEN R. BATTY

IAN ALLAN Publishing

First published 1994

ISBN 0 7110 2236 4

© Ian Allan Ltd 1994

Designed by
David Collins

Published by Ian Allan
Publishing
an imprint of Ian Allan
Ltd, Terminal House,
Station Approach,
Shepperton, Surrey
TW17 8AS; and printed
by Ian Allan Printing Ltd,
Coombelands House,
Coombelands Lane,
Addlestone, Weybridge,
Surrey KT15 1HY.

# Contents

# Introduction

What, another book on Sheffield? — yes, and I make no apologies for having a further look at the once-great railways which crossed within the city of steel! Sheffield was a relatively late starter in matters of railway communication, but developments eventually produced a railway crossroads which contained enough variety and activity to stand comparison with any similar location in the land. The North Midland Railway swept by the city without so much as a by-your-leave, and 30 years were to pass before the Midland Railway built the main line which was so badly needed. Another 25 years passed before the Hope Valley route to Manchester was established. Compare this slothful attitude with that of the Sheffield, Ashton-under-Lyne & Manchester Railway, who built a difficult line across the Pennines, then expanded eastwards to Grimsby and went on to create the Great Central route to London. The resulting network of lines handled vast amounts of traffic, and it was not until relatively recent times that this dwindled away from these levels. Such has been the speed of decline over the last 20 years, however, that these days are rapidly becoming fading memories.

I have once again trawled the archives for a selection of material, and I remain grateful to all those photographers whose work appears here. The city was especially under-photographed during the inter-war years, due, I am reliably informed, to the combination of heavy industrial polution and violent gang warfare — grime and crime — which pervaded the area. Nevertheless, a good selection of prints has been assembled, and I am grateful especially to J. Braithwaite, D. Jackson, B. Longbone, O. Russell, W. T. Stubbs and D. Thompson for their efforts on my behalf. A special vote of thanks must be given to Dr Arthur Barnett, David Pearce and Howard Turner — Dr Barnett's encyclopaedic knowledge of railway building and operation was particularly helpful and he went to great lengths to provide me with information; David Pearce loaned me a generous sample from his treasure trove of railway handbills; and Howard Turner (who, I am sure, has recorded every movement of every wheel in the city since 1948!) once again loaned an excellent collection of negatives, each one packed with interest. Mrs Maxine Robson did her usual excellent job of transforming my sheets of scribble into a superb manuscript, and my wife Andrea gave moral support! Thanks again to everyone.

*Stephen R. Batty*
September 1993

*Front cover:*
*On 7 November 1992 Midland station plays host to two unusual interlopers, Nos 50007 and 50033, who are joined by Class 141 No 141109 dragging the Leeds via Barnsley-Sheffield service.*
Les Nixon

*Front cover, bottom:*
*Ivatt Class 2MT No 46485 pulls away just west of Midland Station with the 0939 Sheffield- Chinley service in June 1966*
P.J. Hughes

*Back cover:*
*Class 47 No 47624 steals away southbound with its Newcastle-Plymouth vans on 2 May 1989*
Les Nixon

TREETON SOUTH

# CHAPTER 1

# From the Early Days to 1870

F

or all its eventual emergence as a crossroads of railway routes and as the centre of the United Kingdom's steel industry, Sheffield's establishment on the railway map was indeed a long-winded affair. An adequate canal connected the town to Doncaster and thence to the navigable Trent, and this would have covered many of the needs for heavy transport of goods to and from Sheffield from the middle of the 18th century up to the dawn of the railway age. The Pennines created a very effective barrier along the western and southern approaches which had deterred canals and good roads for many years, but access to the north and east was unhindered by any such geographical features.

The early 1800s saw many towns grow at unheard-of rates due to industrial expansion, but Sheffield's semi-circular Pennine barrier was effectively cutting the town off precisely in the directions where the greatest markets lay. The mills of Lancashire could be reached only by an expensive and tedious journey via the Peak Forest canal, which itself lay well over 20 miles away. Access to the east was straightforward enough, but this area contained no great industrial markets — Doncaster, Gainsborough, Scunthorpe and the coastal ports barely existed — and was relied upon as a source of agricultural produce. Further north, the industrial area of Leeds and the towns of the Aire and Calder valleys lay along an excellent coast-to-coast waterway network which gave the best heavy industrial transport system seen in the nation prior to the railway age. Sheffield was slumbering well into the 1830s, and even when railway matters finally produced some impact in the area, the first results were not exactly encouraging.

During 1830 moves were made in the right direction when a company was formed to build an eastward extension of the Liverpool & Manchester Railway via Stockport and Whaley Bridge to Sheffield. This Sheffield, Manchester & Liverpool Railway was to be built under the supervision of none other than George and Robert Stephenson, but the route was inflicted with inclined planes, long tunnels and very steep gradients, all of which was very much against the Stephensons' usual practices. On to the scene then stepped Mr Henry Sanderson, a local surveyor who clearly knew his profession well enough to recognise the difference between good and bad railway routes. He proposed instead a more easily-graded route to Manchester via Penistone and Woodhead which required no inclined planes and rather less tunnelling work. Despite tearing the estimates for the costs of the SM&L to shreds, and also putting forward some apparently reasonable figures for the cost of his own scheme, he could not convince the directors of the value of his proposals. By the summer of 1833 the entire project was abandoned.

The year of 1836 was a watershed in the matters of railway communication to the west and south of the town. Two meetings were held, both during January. At the first, a provisional committee for a Sheffield, Ashton-under-Lyne & Manchester Railway (SAMR) was established to build a railway via Deepcar, Wortley and Woodhead, and at the second a surveyor was

*Previous page*
*At the time of the NMR opening in 1840 Treeton was a small, isolated village along the route which could boast several small coal mines in the area. The traffic was catered for by a station being opened in the locality, but this was closed by January 1843 and it was not until October 1884 that the replacement was provided. Final closure took place in October 1951, and Class 40 No 40178 is seen passing the site on 27 February 1982 with a Redcar-Corby steel coil train.*

*A. Taylor*

appointed to consider a direct railway route to Chesterfield. The SAMR was successfully promoted after the infant Liverpool & Manchester had clearly shown what could be done with locomotive power in terms of reliability and haulage capacity. Not too far to the north, the Leeds & Selby Railway had opened in 1834 and was enjoying great success with passenger and goods traffic, and the promoters —representing industrial interests on both sides of the Pennines— clearly felt confident enough to tackle the problems of crossing the hills to the west. No lesser persons than Joseph Locks and Charles Vignoles were given the task of engineering a route which closely followed Sanderson's original proposals, terminating in a station at Bridgehouses, near the cattle market. The SAMR received their Act in May 1837, but work did not start until October of the following year, when the first spadeful was lifted from the barren, windswept Salter's Brook high on the Woodhead Pass.

The second meeting of January 1836 was brought about by the declaration of the proposed North Midland Railway that their route from London, Rugby and Derby to Leeds would pass by Sheffield completely, pausing only at Rotherham, in order to keep the gradients to a minimum. Both Vignoles and George Hudson tried to persuade Stephenson to divert the NMR into Sheffield, but to no avail. Independent proposals were made to establish a direct Chesterfield line, but visions of spectacular earthworks deterred the investors and instead pushed support towards an alternative plan to build a short line from near the Wicker, along the Don valley through Meadow Hall and to a terminus at Rotherham. A short spur would connect into the NMR main line at Masbrough, giving Sheffield a sort of 'shunt' access to this magnificent main line proposal. Locke had stated that the SAMR would certainly extend eastwards in the near future towards Gainsborough and Lincoln, but no amount of lobbying could produce a direct access route to the south.

*Right:*
*George Stephenson's North Midland route was engineered to avoid steep gradients, which meant denying any access to Sheffield because of the steep descent needed on any direct approach from Chesterfield. Consequently, the line was laid along a falling route between Chesterfield and Rotherham where the gradient was no steeper than 1 in 308. Class 37 No 37049 Imperial is here seen at the northern end of the section, approaching Masbrough station with a down ballast train on 19 March 1993.*
*S. R. Batty*

The Sheffield & Rotherham Railway received their Act in July 1836 and started work in January 1837. Opening took place in November 1838, finally placing Sheffield on the railway map even if the new branch line did expire somewhat suddenly at Rotherham. The NMR was still under construction at this time, and it was not until May 1840 that travel to Derby, Birmingham and London became possible. Connection to Leeds, York and Hull was made in July of the same year, and at last it seemed that Sheffield was set to enjoy the benefits of decent railway communication, even if the system was far from complete. The little S&RR was rather too small to survive in the face of poor economic conditions and the predatory eyes of bigger neighbours; the depression of 1842/43 weakened the company and halted plans to extend across town to meet the SAMR near Bridgehouses , and in 1844 George Hudson's newly-created Midland Railway was seen by the directors as the company saviour. Terms were agreed, and the S&RR became part of the Hudson empire from July 1845 .

Although some economies had to be made to the original SAMR scheme almost before the ink was dry on the 1837 Act, other promoters lost no time in using the Sheffield terminus as a springboard for newly planned routes out of the town. A very early proposal to reach Nottingham quickly sank, but a scheme of 1838 to reach the North Midland Railway at Woodhouse Mill set the pattern for future expansion out of Bridgehouses before it, too, came to nothing. Not until 1844 was any real progress made, when one Henry Hinde took the floor at a public meeting to discuss yet another line to Chesterfield and put forward his own alternative of building eastwards to Gainsborough and Lincoln and using connections with the new London & York Railway to reach the capital. It worked — Sheffield & Lincolnshire Junction Railway was formed on 7 March 1844 and received its Act on 3 August 1846. The intervening period witnessed the last pre-1870 attempts to reach Chesterfield and also one or two alternative eastbound proposals, but the SAMR quickly allied itself with the new SLJR and successfully fought off all such plans, especially those which had backing from the Manchester & Leeds Railway. (The M&LR was the SAMR's principal competitor for trans-Pennine traffic and also had clear ambitions of extending eastwards.)

The SAMR opened, without very much public fuss, on 12 July 1845. Passengers had to travel by road from Dunford Bridge to Woodhead until the tunnel was finished in December, but Sheffield's branch-line status was at an end. The SAMR opening took place just ten days before the Midland Railway took over the S&RR, and as if to further emphasise the end of the era, coincidence saw to it that in the same month work started on building the half-mile connection from Wicker through Spital Hill tunnel to meet the Manchester line at Bridgehouses. This short line was expected to provide the SAMR with a great deal of traffic, and together with that to be provided by the SLJR, was thought to be too much for Bridgehouses to handle. Work on the SLJR officially started at

*Continued on page 12*

*Right:*
*Work on the Sheffield &
Rotherham Railway is
recorded as having started in
a garden at Brightside. This
1947 view of the station
shows the results of a
century's development, with
long platforms, loops around
the platform roads and
recent brick buildings.*
D. Thompson

*Right:*
*The S&RR terminus at
Wicker was close to the town
centre, but always suffered
from being physically
cramped and unable to be
developed to take greater
amounts of traffic. Even
after conversion into a goods
depot, the problems
remained. This view, taken
on 13 May 1912, shows the
yard in full swing with
barely any spare capacity
available.*
NRM - Crown
Copyright Reserved

*Right:*
*At the other end of Sheffield
branch the S&RR station
was built near Westgate,
and a spur was built to
connect into the NMR main
line near Masborough
station. The connection was
greatly enlarged over the
following years, and this
view, taken on 20 December
1920, shows the
Masborough Station South
Junction signalbox, the
Control Office building
within the V of the junction
and the extensive sidings
and pointwork laid in the
area.*
NRM - Crown
Copyright Reserved

*Right:*
*By the way of a contrast this view, taken almost 60 years later on 3 September 1980, shows the great reduction of trackwork which had taken place relatively recently. The former Control Office survives as a silent witness to the passing of 'Peak' Class 46 No 46032 with the 17.35 Leeds-Sheffield service.*
                    Brian Morrison

*Right:*
*The SAMR route to Manchester took trains westwards over a long climb to the distant summit at Woodhead, but the chosen route was engineered to avoid the vicious gradients of some of the earlier schemes which had been proposed. Class 76 No 76040 leaves the sidings at Stocksbridge Steelworks and descends the 1 in 120 through Deepcar towards Sheffield on 7 July 1981.*
                    A. G. Castle

*Right:*
*Traffic across the Pennines rapidly built up to the levels hoped for by the SAMR directors, and in the years around the turn of the century many loops and sidings had to be built. Class B8 4-6-0 No 5445 is seen passing the Neepsend loops with a Blackpool excursion in 1936.*
                    A. G. Ellis Collection

*Right:*
*Despite never being known as one of the country's more magnificent railway establishments, Victoria station was certainly an improvement on the S&RR's Wicker terminus and did not need any radical alterations for nearly 60 years. A two-car DMU departs from platform 4 towards Doncaster on 10 April 1965.*
D. S. Frith

*Right:*
*The fearsomely-inclined Spital Hill tunnel line was built to provide a connection through from Wicker station on to the SAMR west of Bridgehouses. Goods traffic was handled for many years, but the improvement of other yards eventually led to its decline. This 1950 view of the SAMR end shows the poor state of the approaches after more than a century of use.*
D. Ibbotson

*Right:*
*Attempts were first made to build a station at Neepsend in 1857, but the cost of bridging the River Don dissuaded the MSLR from committing themselves. Eventually Sheffield Corporation agreed to pay £1900 for excavations and buildings, and the station opened in July 1888. Life was short, however, and the station had been closed for eight years when this 1948 view was taken.*

Darnall in October and went ahead at a brisk pace — a new station had to be put in hand quickly, and plans were made to build arches across the Wicker into a brand-new station which would handle SAMR/SLJR traffic for the foreseeable future. Not surprisingly, the two companies amalgamated from 1 January 1847 as the Manchester, Sheffield & Lincolnshire Railway, thus fulfilling Joseph Locke's assurance of 1836 that any railway from Manchester to Sheffield would certainly be extended towards the east coast. Due to the large amount of civil engineering required at Wicker and at Beighton viaduct, it was not until February 1849 that public services started running eastwards from Bridgehouses and the opening of the new station — Victoria — did not take place until September 1851.

Sheffield's last piece of railway construction in the years before 1870 took place largely at the instigation of the little-known, but very ambitious, South Yorkshire Railway. The SYR was essentially concerned with hauling coal from Barnsley towards the east coast ports and also to London via the MR or GNR, but from 1847 the little company decided that the Midland branch into Wicker station would provide a suitable extension for their existing passenger services between Doncaster and Barnsley. A Doncaster-Swinton-Wicker service started from November 1849, but two years later work started on the Blackburn Valley line from Aldam Junction, between Mexborough and Barnsley, to a point known as Blackburn Valley Junction on the MR main line between Brightside and Wincobank. When finally opened in September 1854, this allowed the running of a direct Wicker-Chapeltown-Barnsley service, so avoiding the previous changing at Swinton. The Wicker station soon became overcrowded, and the Midland Railway probably preferred to handle the large amount of goods traffic without interference from the SYR's passenger trains, which had to be fitted in amongst the company's own Rotherham service workings.

By 1861 the SYR was building its own line into Sheffield from Meadow Hall Junction, on the Barnsley line, to a planned station near the canal basin. In return for a decent share of the coal traffic, the MSLR offered the SYR the use of Victoria station, access to which was to be gained by bringing the new SYR line into the MSLR at Woodburn Junction, to the east of Victoria. The South Yorkshire accepted the offer and went away to build the line, but the company had their own ideas about buying land, obtaining Acts of Parliament and indeed about all matters connected with the legalities of actually constructing a railway. These ideas could be generally summed up as '... never mind about the rights and wrongs, let's get on with it!' Nevertheless, the arguments, threats and general wrangling delayed the opening until 1 August 1864, when the MSLR took over the SYR and the Barnsley service was transferred to Victoria from Wicker. Only one intermediate station was provided, at Broughton Lane, but stations followed at Tinsley and Attercliffe in 1869 and 1871 respectively.

The SYR had taken over the River Don Navigation Co in 1850,

*Right:*
*Neepsend loco survived until Darnall was opened in 1943, and played host to all manner of MSLR/GCR/LNER motive power. One of the graceful Robinson Class 8B Atlantics (LNER Class C4), No 6094, is seen on shed in the 1930s.*
B. R. Longbone Collection

*Right:*
*The MR line to Barnsley left the former S&RR at Wincobank Station Junction, between Brightside and Wincobank stations. A Class 123 DMU is seen here in July 1978 passing the remodelled junction layout with a Hull-Manchester train. The Barnsley lines can be seen in the foreground, with the new 'ladder' arrangement for Barnsley-Sheffield trains clearly visible.*
T. Dodgson

*Right:*
*A Leeds-Barnsley-Sheffield DMU rejoins the main line at Wincobank Station Junction, leaving the 1893-built MR Barnsley connection. Immediately behind the train can be seen the severed remains of the SYR Blackburn Valley Junction, closed to passenger traffic in 1953. Wincobank station, which closed to passengers in 1956, was situated between this junction and the semaphore signal just beyond the box. The viaduct above the SYR line carried the 1894-built connection between Wincobank North and West Junctions.*
T.Dodgson

**14**

thus giving the MSLR a ready route along which to build a new line from Tinsley to Rotherham and gain much better access to the coalfield. The MSLR promptly started work in 1864, but the need to buy land (in spite of its being supposedly owned by the SYR!) and divert the waterway and build new locks soon saw the expenditure soaring. Opening to a temporary station at Rotherham finally took place in August 1868, and it was not until February 1874 that this was rebuilt into Rotherham Central station. Curiously, this last piece of MSLR main-line construction had scuppered an approved plan to build into Sheffield from Chapel-en-le-Frith along the Hope Valley.

The London & North Western Railway had received an Act for such a scheme, but had been approached by the MSLR when money for the Rotherham line was rapidly drying up. The LNWR already had running powers from Manchester to Victoria, but had never used these to any great extent. The MSLR urged the LNWR to use their powers to the full and also take a joint share in the Rotherham line, which was bound to pay a good return in coal traffic. The catch was quite simple — the LNWR must drop the Hope Valley route. It was too good a scheme to miss, as the LNWR could gain good access to Sheffield at virtually no cost, apart perhaps from sharing the bill for any improvements needed at Victoria, and the Rotherham line would surely pay off. Parliament, however, was not so impressed, and threw out the Bill.

The LNWR route would not have done a great deal for better access to London, but it would have taken a railway along the steep southern exit from the town centre and made extension on towards Chesterfield a straightforward business. The Hope Valley line had to wait 25 years before becoming a reality.

*Above:*
MSLR ambitions in the Rotherham area were started by the joint building with the SYR of the line from Meadowhall Junction to Woodburn Junction, eventually opened in August 1864. Construction from Tinsley through to Rotherham was completed exactly four years later. Broughton Lane was the only intermediate station ready for the 1864 opening, with Tinsley and Attercliffe following in March 1869 and August 1871 respectively. This 1947 view of Broughton Lane, looking towards Sheffield, shows a well-equipped station but very little traffic or passengers. Closure took place in April 1956.

D. Thompson

*Below:*
A view of City Goods depot, the ex-LNWR establishment of 1903 at Wharf Street, taken on 28 August 1925. The three-floored building can be seen behind the yard, with the hydraulic tower used for operating the wagon lifts being clearly visible. Two lifts could raise and lower 20-ton loads between rail and street level, but the lack of traffic in the yard suggests business was slack by the mid-1920s.

NRM — Crown Copyright Reserved

# CHAPTER 2

# Completion of the System, 1870-1900

The Midland's so-called service from Sheffield to London stagnated throughout a 25-year period, giving an inadequate service from the Wicker (which was more of a goods yard than a passenger station) to Masbrough, where connections were unreliable and waits were often apparently endless. Agitation for a direct Chesterfield line resumed in earnest from late 1862, and the MR realised they could not turn a deaf ear. Alternative schemes were beginning to surface, and a public meeting held in December resulted in an independent company being formed in order to keep the MR under pressure until the line was completed. The MR was the preferred company, but Derby was left in no doubts that any contractor would be welcomed who could provide the long-overdue southern exit. By the summer of 1863 the Midland had drawn up the necessary plans, including a station above the Sheaf near Harmer Lane, and Parliamentary approval was expected to follow in the 1864 Session. Despite this apparently happy conclusion, there then emerged another alternative scheme, heavily backed by several local industrialists, to build southwards to Chesterfield and then across country to meet the LNWR at Stafford. Naturally, the Midland was somewhat put out by this act of treachery from yet another faction of the Sheffield party, but the Stafford line failed due to unconvincing cost estimates and some fly-by-night financing methods.

Work started quickly and went ahead at a good pace, but public services from Tapton Junction (near Chesterfield, on what became known as the 'Old Road') to Grimesthorpe Junction (where the original S&R was joined) did not start until February 1870. Passenger services were finally removed from the miserable station at Wicker, and new local stations were built at Abbey Houses, Ecclesall, Heeley and Attercliffe Road. The whole episode must have left the Midland feeling rather nonplussed. The new station, often known somewhat erroneously as Pond Street, was criticised for being placed in a very unsalubrious part of town and also for having dangerously unfinished approach roads. No public ceremony of any sort marked the opening, and the buildings themselves were not received with overwhelming enthusiasm. But the Midland had the trump card — the Settle and Carlisle was under way, and Sheffield would soon be on a brand-new Anglo-Scottish trunk route which was certain to generate large amounts of passenger and freight traffic.

Over 20 years then passed before the MR completed their last ventures in the Sheffield area. The independent Dore & Chinley Railway was formed to build westwards from the 1872-built Dore & Totley station across the Pennines to Chinley, but unfortunately failed to generate enough share capital and was only too pleased when MR stepped in and took over the company. Passengers finally started using the line in June 1894, when the tunnels at Totley and Cowburn were eventually completed. Civil engineering practices had improved tremendously since the days of the early ventures at Woodhead, Summit and Standedge, but these two features had shown that nature still had a very strong hand to play.

*Previous page:*
*Shed workshop facilities were often very comprehensive, Grimesthorpe had the ability to completely strip and rebuild locomotives on site. This scene, also posed for the benefit of the MR photographer on 14 July 1920, shows the use of the depot's shear legs.*
NRM — Crown Copyright Reserved

*Continued on page 22*

*Right:*
*Robinson's first 4-6-0 design was the Class 8 machine, 14 being built between 1902 and 1904. Running as LNER Class B5, No 6069 is seen as Neepsend alongside ex-GNR Atlantic No 4412, one of 10 of the 'C1' class which were allocated here from 1923 onwards.*
B. R. Longbone
Collection

*Right:*
*At the Grouping of 1923 the LNER Class D9 4-4-0s (the former GCR Classes 11B, 11C and 11D) were the largest passenger locomotives based at Sheffield. No 5111, a Class 11D variant, is seen here at Neepsend in post-1925 condition.*
B. R. Longbone
Collection

*Right:*
*Robinson's Class 11E 4-4-0 was an extremely powerful and well-liked machine which could handle fast trains towards Nottingham or pound up the climb to Woodhead. No 5433* Walter Burgh Gair *is seen at Neepsend in April 1939, when the entire class of 10 locomotives was allocated there for a short period.*
D. Jackson Collection

*Right:*
*The Royal Victoria Hotel was built adjacent to Victoria station and was taken over by the MSLR in late 1889. Its dignified appearance always overwhelmed the railway station, but by this April 1993 view the station has been completely demolished and replaced by a Holiday Inn directly on the trackbed. The remaining single line to Stockbridge steelworks runs behind the new building.*
S.R.Batty

*Right:*
*Robinson's Class 11F 4-4-0 locomotives were introduced from 1919, and the class eventually totalled 35 machines after the LNER built a batch of 24 from 1924 onwards. Production of the class was prompted by the failure of the 1917-built 'Lord Faringdon' 4-6-0s to live up to expectations, and the new locos were very similar to their designer's earlier '11E' machines. No 5509, built in March 1920 and seen here running as LNER Class D11, enters Victoria from the east on 14 September 1929.*
W. L. Good

*Right:*
*The class B18 totalled just two locomotives, Nos 5195 and 5196. These had been built in 1903/4 for comparison purposes with 4-4-2s Nos 192 and 194, and Robinson concluded that the Atlantic class was the better performer. No 5196 is seen here entering Victoria on 15 June 1935, probably hauling a Banbury-Sheffield train during the period when No 5196 was allocated to Woodford. She was withdrawn in December 1947.*
A. G. Ellis Collection

*Right:*
Both exits from the Midland Railway station were extremely gloomy; this view of the northbound exit demonstrates the point well. The main lines to and from Rotherham are on the left, with the Nunnery Curve line climbing steeply away to the right. The lower-level bridge carries the Nunnery Colliery lines and the higher structure carries the 1895 LNWR branch from Woodburn Junction into the City Goods depot in Bernard Road. Nunnery Main Line Junction signalbox can be seen below the bridges.

D. Ibbotson

*Right:*
Wincobank station lay amidst the maze of junctions between the MR and GCR lines to Barnsley, Rotherham and Sheffield. Named Wincobank at its 1868 opening, the station was renamed Wincobank & Meadow Hall in July 1899 before reverting to its original title from June 1951. Plenty of staff and passengers are apparent in this 1947 view, which also manages to convey an almost rustic impression more appropriate to a branch line station.

D. Thompson

*Right:*
Wicker station saw many years of active use as a busy city-centre goods depot before eventual closure in July 1965. This view, taken on 7 September 1922, shows a procession of horse-drawn carts leaving the Saville Street entrance (possibly arranged for the photographer), a fine Sheffield tram, a steam road locomotive and a solitary car.
NRM — Crown Copyright Reserved

Nearer the town, the Midland built a short branch from the former S&R line at Wincobank up to Thorncliffe Ironworks which opened in August 1893 and had a north-facing connection (ie towards Rotherham) added in 1896. By the following year the line was extended to Barnsley, and a full passenger service commenced from 1 July. The line ran almost side by side with the 1854 South Yorkshire line, but was ultimately destined to see a much longer life.

The 1890s saw three further pieces of railway work started, and the most important of these was the MSLR's line from Beighton to Annesley, near Nottingham. A branch was included towards Chesterfield, but the real reason for the new construction was to make a start at building a brand-new main line from the north to London. The MSLR was expanding its colliery lines in the Derbyshire area and Annesley was a good location for exchange of coal traffic. It also gave them access, via GNR lines, into Nottingham. Opening took place in 1892, but several years had to pass and a good many battles had to be won before Marylebone was reached.

This expansion of coal traffic did not go unnoticed by the LNWR. Using their running powers from Manchester, the LNWR quickly began to run coal traffic between here and Annesley, abandoning their earlier practice of exchanging loads at Doncaster. They even built a goods depot at Bernard Road, known as City Goods and opened in May 1895. Access was via a 3/4-mile branch eastwards from Woodburn Junction. Eight years later the company opened an improved depot at the junction of Broad Street and Wharf Street, reached from the Bernard Road branch by extending beneath the Nunnery Colliery Railway and then continuing above the MR's northern exit. A small locomotive shed was also included. To avoid confusion, the new depot took over the title of City Goods and the old depot was renamed Nunnery Goods, where the heavier loads continued to be handled.

The third development of the 1890s brought another geographically-remote company into the city when the Great Eastern Railway gained running powers over the Sheffield District Railway, opened in May 1900. The story began in the later 1880s when proposals were first made for a new railway to run right across the country from Warrington to Sutton-on-Sea in Lincolnshire. Plans had long been laid for new docks at the eastern end of the route, and the line was primarily intended to give the coal owners good access to two ports for export of their coal. It was a massive scheme involving some 170 miles of new railway, including what would have been a truly spectacular 300ft high viaduct across Monsal Dale in Derbyshire. Known as the Lancashire, Derbyshire & East Coast Railway, it had not a friend in the world when the plans were made public, and the MSLR was a particularly aggressive opponent. The GER, however, had for many years sought a way to break into the lucrative coal trade, and quickly stepped forward with support. (Traffic could be connected into the GER system via the GNR/GER joint line at Pyewipe

Continued on page 26

*Right:*
*The Sheffield District Railway's origins were tangled with the formation of the Lancashire, Derbyshire & East Coast Railway and with the Great Eastern Railway's ambitions towards the hauling of coal traffic. Opened in 1900, the 3$^{1}$/$_{2}$-mile system never achieved traffic levels which could justify the cost involved in building the line. This January 1911 view shows a Midland Railway 0-4-4T passing Grimesthorpe at District Railway Junction with a northbound local service heading towards Rotherham. The SDR line can be seen on the left, with access to Attercliffe Goods curving away opposite the train.*
NRM — Crown
Copyright Reserved

*Right:*
*Millhouses locomotive shed supplied the power for passenger workings out of Sheffield. This view, taken on 27 April 1910, shows a very tidy yard area with only two locos on view.*
NRM — Crown
Copyright Reserved

*Right:*
*Grimesthorpe MPD was very much concerned with the freight business, and this well-posed scene shows a pair of '3F' 0-6-0s being coaled and watered on 14 July 1920. No 3147 is cleaned to perfection, and even the inside of the loco coal barrow is spotless!*
NRM — Crown
Copyright Reserved

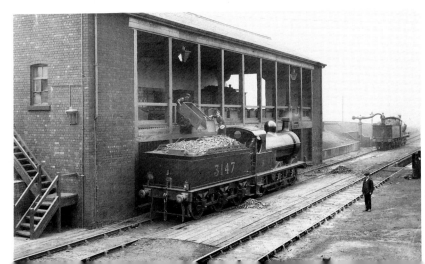

*Above:*
Sharp Stewart-built 4-4-0 No 2212 is seen at the Midland station. This locomotive was new in 1893 and renumbered 437 in 1907 prior to withdrawal in 1914.

L&GRP/Ian Allan Library

*Below:*
The Midland station at Sheffield in 1904, just prior to the extensive rebuilding which created extra platform space to the right of this scene. Quadrupling of the tracks to the south, at the far end of the station, would have been completed by this time.

NRM — Crown Copyright Reserved

*Top:*
*Class O4 No 5415 is pictured at Neepsend in 1931.*
*Designed by Robinson and introduced in 1911, the ex-*
*Great Central 2-8-0s were constructed for freight work.*
L&GRP/Ian Allan Library

*Above:*
*Queens Road goods depot on 13 May 1912. Despite being*
*very busy, the yard is clean and tidy — perhaps the*
*impending visit of the photographer led to a rapid clean-up*
*campaign! The painter has certainly been busy, judging by*
*the immaculate cabin window frames, cattle-pen fencing*
*and trackwork point handles.*
NRM — Crown Copyright Reserved

Junction, Lincoln). Amazingly, the LDECR received their Act in July 1891, and the MSLR must have been furious at the approval also for a short branch northwards from Langwith to Beighton to allow the local collieries to be connected.

Unfortunately, the promoters' enthusiasm was not matched by a suitable level of capital donations, and the scheme quickly ground to a halt. The GER then took full control and directed that only the central section from Chesterfield to Lincoln should be built, together with the Beighton branch. Work started in 1892 (still with 'Lancashire' in the title — the GER perhaps hoped to satisfy the 'East Coast' implications!) and was completed in 1897. The Beighton connection was actually tied into the MR main line at that point, and a group of Sheffield businessmen then formed their own company in order to extend the LDECR directly into the city. The LDECR was short of cash and could offer only moral support, the GER did not want to risk any more money against what they saw as only a marginal gain, and the MSLR was as hostile as ever. Fortunately, the MR was approachable, and plans were made to use running powers along the 1840 'Old Road' to Treeton and from a new junction at Brightside into the Midland station in the city.

This left only a short Treeton-Brightside section to be built, along with a short branch into a new goods depot at Attercliffe, reached also from the MR at Sheffield District Junction. The new company was known as the Sheffield District Railway, and construction took place between 1896 and 1900. Although only $3^1/2$ miles in length, the Treeton-Brightside line was a succession of viaducts, girder bridges, cuttings, one tunnel and a vast amount of infilling and river diversion work. The Attercliffe goods depot was a monumental work which could never have hoped to provide a decent return on the capital which it swallowed up. The goods traffic did not materialise, and the passenger services (operated from the MR station by the LDECR to Langwith, and also from 1903 by the MR themselves to Mansfield) were also poor. By 1905 the directors were looking for a buyer, but the hoped-for buyers — the Midland and the Great Eastern — were not interested. Eventually, in 1907, the system was bought out by none other than the Great Central Railway, the 1897 successor to the LDECR's principal foe, the MSLR.

The years around the turn of the century saw many improvements to both the MR and GCR stations in the town centre, and also to the main-line trackwork. The Midland's goods depots were improved, but the principal passenger station at Pond Street remained a somewhat humble affair compared to some of the company's other establishments. Fearing that matters might be left to drift along in the complacency which seemed to surround Midland passenger affairs at Sheffield, a group of regular railway users wrote to express their dissatisfaction to the MR management. The reply, from none other than the chairman, Sir Ernest Paget, stated that no less than £800,000 was due to be spent in the area, including £216,000 on the station itself. When it was finally completed in 1905, the rebuilt station was still regarded as rather a non-event in architectural terms, but the facilities for travellers were greatly improved. The essential features were the provision of two new through platforms and two new bays, achieved by widening the station in a westerly direction. New offices were built, facing on to Sheaf Street, and six footbridges were provided — four for passengers and two for luggage and mail traffic.

These station improvements went hand-in-hand with a scheme to widen all the permanent way as far south as Dore & Totley. This need had been apparent for some time, as the steady procession of coal trains climbing the bank — and also the return empty workings to the Barnsley coalfield — was jamming the line and threatening to cause serious delays to the passenger traffic. The original double track was to serve the Manchester traffic and a new double track layout, built alongside and to the east, would take the Derby and London trains. To allow the principal express trains to use the new platforms on the western side of the station, a burrowing junction was dug out near Queens Road goods depot. More arches above the Sheaf were built to make room for the new trackwork, and the tunnel at the southern approach to the station was opened out. New island platforms were added at the stations along the route — Heeley, Millhouses & Ecclesall, Beauchief & Abbeydale, and also at Dore & Totley. The work was completed by 1902, well before the station improvements were finished.

Developments on the GCR services followed a very similar pattern, resulting in some improvements at Victoria station and the elimination of bottlenecks in the main line approaches. Apart from the general increase in traffic levels which took place during the 1890s, the new Marylebone services (which started in April 1899) added a further load which almost choked the lines from Victoria to Woodhouse. The MSLR had granted running powers to the GNR over Woodhead as long ago as 1873, and these had been reinforced by the MSLR as a 'sweetener' to buy off any GNR opposition to the planned London extension scheme. Consequently, by the turn of the century Victoria was having to cope with not only the GCR's new London traffic, but also a healthy GNR London-Manchester-Liverpool service as well. Something had to be done, and the answers lay in a widening scheme from Victoria through Woodburn Junction and Darnall to Handsworth tunnel, and then from the eastern exit through to a point just beyond Woodhouse, where the Retford and London lines parted company. The work was completed for less than £80,000 after approval in 1900, but of course the biggest bottleneck of all was left untouched in the form of Handsworth tunnel. This curious state of affairs was to last until 1913, when the tunnel was eventually opened out and further track improvements were carried out at both Darnall and Woodhouse. Looking westwards, long goods loops were built at Neepsend and Woodhead during 1895/96, but it was not until 1909 that Bridgehouses tunnel was removed to allow more widening to be done in the goods depot area. Victoria station was developed in rather a piecemeal fashion, with the principal alteration being the extension of the arches below the station and the realignment of

Sussex Street allow a through goods line to be built on the north side of the layout. A new 290yd platform was thus gained and the existing bay platforms were lengthened. A new frontage and subway were added, but it was left to the adjacent Royal Victoria hotel to add any visual impact to the scene.

The Edwardian era saw great improvements in long-distance railway passenger travel through faster schedules, better rolling stock and new services, and Sheffield was placed on a railway crossroads which saw some of the best of the new developments. As far as the Midland Railway was concerned the city was ideally placed on their Anglo-Scottish trunk route between St Pancras and Glasgow for tapping into traffic from the northeast and the West Riding conurbation. Good services reached into the southwest via Birmingham to Bristol, and the Hope Valley route gave an excellent way into Manchester, with some trains attaching or detaching Liverpool portions at Chinley. Several Scottish services bypassed the city altogether by using the direct Rotherham-Chesterfield line, and slip coaches were regularly used to provide a Sheffield connection from Masbrough.

The Midland main line to St Pancras was not laid out for speed and could not compete on this count with the GCR's brand-new London Extension, but the MR trains were well known for comfort and excellent dining car facilities. The West Riding services were among the Midland's best, and a new route was opened up from July 1909 when traffic began using the Royston-Thornhill line to reach Bradford and Halifax by courtesy of the Lancashire & Yorkshire Railway (who also provided most of the motive power) along the Calder Valley. A further inter-company service concerned Hull, which was served by two trains daily each way operated jointly by the MR and the North Eastern Railway. Not to be outdone, the Hull & Barnsley Railway provided six trains daily between Pond Street and Cannon Street, but taking 115min instead of the MR/NER 105min. The northeast-southwest services connected Newcastle and York with Bristol, Exeter, Bournemouth, Torquay and Plymouth, with most trains using the 1879-opened Swinton & Knottingley Joint line to avoid congestion at Normanton. Several of these trains also used slip coaches to serve Rotherham on their non-stop runs between Sheffield and York. The Great Central's Marylebone services amounted to seven or eight trains daily each way during the years after the opening of the new line. The number of trains varied slightly from year to year and this fairly low total was bolstered by the GNR's three return trips worked every day between Victoria and King's Cross. Two of these worked through to or from Manchester, the remaining up train starting from Sheffield after having a carriage attached from a Liverpool-Cleethorpes service, and the last down train terminated at Victoria at 2.45am. Although the GCR never achieved a reputation for outright speed, as accomplished by the GNR on the East Coast main line, they did produce some extremely rapid running with the 'Sheffield Specials' from 1903 onwards. In July of that year a return non-stop Victoria-Marylebone service was introduced which took 3hr 10min going up and only 3hr 8min coming down. Three months later both times were cut to three hours dead, and in July 1904 the journey was cut to 2hr 57min at the same time as the train was extended to Manchester and given a slip portion for Penistone. The trains were very lightly-loaded — initially only to three coaches — and were hauled by a 4-4-0 locomotive, but the new Robinson Atlantic 4-4-2s were used as the train weights increased.

Having spent a vast sum on building their new main line to London, the Great Central chose to exploit it not so much through speed as through the provision of cross-country services between virtually all points of the compass. The chairman, Sam Fay, had to make the line pay in the face of long-established rivals who would do all they could to protect their own routes from the north to the capital, and he developed the GCR-operated cross-country routes by using two weapons — running agreements and publicity. His principal partners were the North Eastern and Great Western railways, with the London & South Western and South Eastern & Chatham companies playing additional roles. Publicity was actively promoted amongst the travelling public, and the GCR quickly acquired a reputation for innovative and effective advertising. The new services were introduced progressively from 1900, with a Newcastle/Sunderland-Southampton/Bournemouth train, and three years later a Manchester-Dover working was introduced. Through carriages were worked from the West Riding to Bristol from 1904, and 1906 saw Sheffield-Cardiff and York-Cardiff services started, with the latter including a Newcastle coach.

The same year saw improvements to the company's services which connected with ferry sailings to continental Europe. Since 1885 the GER had operated a service from Harwich to Birmingham, York and Manchester, but the intervening 20 years had not seen any great improvement in the train's running. During 1906 a modern set of six bogie cars was built at Stratford for the service, and the 'North Country Continental' underwent a revival. After leaving Peterborough, where a Birmingham portion was detached, the train ran across the Fens to Lincoln, from where the GER took one portion to York and the GCR took the remainder on to Sheffield. From Victoria the train was divided yet again, travelling attached to two separate trains to Manchester and Liverpool. The Great Central's 'own' port of Grimsby was blessed with a service from Manchester which ran on Tuesdays, Thursdays and Saturdays and connected with steamers to Europe, with the return workings connecting with the arriving boats on the following days. The trains were extended to Liverpool in 1909, giving a true cross-country service.

*Above:*
*Turn-of-the-century improvements at Victoria consisted essentially of building a new goods line on the north side of the platforms and making slight alterations to the bay platforms and down main line. This August 1978 view clearly shows the later goods line curving round the station, together with the Royal Victoria Hotel and remains of Blast Lane goods yard on the left.*

D. Pearce

*Right:*
*A closer view of the extension above Suffolk Street, taken during the last months of passenger operation. Class EM1 No E26055 Prometheus heads eastwards with empties on 3 September 1969.*

V. Bamford

# CHAPTER 3
# The Post-Grouping Years

Sheffield's railway story between Grouping and Nationalisation was broadly characterised by depression and times of war. Although the city's railways were taken over by two companies which constantly vied each other for records of speed and quality of service, neither the London, Midland & Scottish Railway nor the London & North Eastern Railway paid very much attention to their Sheffield services in terms of speed, frequency or quality. The city lay between the West Coast and East Coast routes, and the former Midland route to Leeds, Carlisle and Glasgow had never enjoyed any reputation for sheer speed such as could be achieved by the rival routes from London to Glasgow and Edinburgh. A brief renaissance took place during the 1920s, when a 3hr 10min Marylebone service was introduced with stops at Leicester and Nottingham and also including a Penistone call during the Manchester connection. The ex-GCR 'Director' 4-4-0 locos performed well on this return service, but the new Class B17 4-6-0s took over when the train was lengthened to include a Bradford portion.

The King's Cross service reappeared in June 1924 (after disappearing in 1916) with the introduction of the 'Sheffield Pullman', which took the ex-GNR route to Nottingham before going on to Victoria over former GCR lines. The journey took only five minutes longer than the 'rival' Marylebone service, but very little custom was attracted and revisions were made during the following month. Running times were altered and the service was reversed to give an arrival in London at 1.45pm and a departure at 6.5pm, but all to no avail. The Nottingham stop was removed and the train extended to Manchester to try and improve custom, but even a speeding-up to 2hr 57min via Retford from Victoria failed to do the trick. The Pullman was withdrawn in autumn 1925, the train set being put to use on the 'West Riding Pullman'.

Just prior to this, the LMSR introduced their St Pancras-Sheffield-Bradford service in March 1925, known unofficially as the 'Yorkshireman'. Revenue was good and a second train was eventually put on in 1937, with the time to Sheffield coming down to 2hr 52min. These trains disappeared in September 1939, along with the 3hr 10min Marylebone trains, and it was to be many a long year before services to the capital even approached such speeds. Three LMSR trains introduced during 1927 were destined to have extremely long lives, surviving the 1939-45 period and going on well past eventual Nationalisation in 1948. Two of these were Anglo-Scottish services and the third was a West Riding-West of England working; they were the 'Thames-Clyde Express', the 'Thames-Forth Express' (later known as 'The Waverley') and the 'Devonian'. The 'Thames-Forth' left St Pancras at 9.5am and indulged in some fast running to Nottingham before subsidence slowed affairs down. After leaving a Halifax coach at Sheffield, the train went on to Leeds for reversal before attacking the climb to Blea Moor, and ultimately reaching Edinburgh via the Waverley route. In these prewar years the train was limited to only seven coaches, hauled by nothing grander than MR/LMSR 4-4-0s until

*Previous page:*
*The Midland Railway's 'small engine' policy lasted well beyond 1923; in the following year the LMSR produced a brand-new series of Class 4P Compound 4-4-0 locomotives based almost entirely on the earlier MR product. Resplendent No 1091 is seen at Grimesthorpe on 1 May 1932, when still a relatively new engine.*

*W. L. Good*

the new 'Jubilee' 4-6-0s arrived to bestow a little more power and dignity on the scene. The war years saw 2½-3½hr added on to the 9¼hr up and 8¾hr down journeys, and through working to Edinburgh being replaced by a single coach added to Glasgow workings.

After October 1945 speeds were slowly raised, but it was not until 1957 that any great improvement was made. Speeds were generally restored to the 1939 level, and the train was renamed as the 'Waverley' to run during the summer months only — during winter, the service was cut back to an unnamed Leeds/Bradford run. Twelve years later the title disappeared when the Carlisle-Edinburgh 'Waverley' route was closed.

The 'Thames-Clyde Express' followed a similar course through history, giving a St Pancras-Glasgow service which ran throughout 1939-45 and eventually petered out in the mid-1970s. Initially, the down train ran via the Old Road and bypassed Sheffield, with only the up service pausing in the city at approximately 7.25pm. Until 1937 this train dropped a Nottingham portion at Trent, but this stop, together with the harder climb needed out of Sheffield, caused considerable slowing and was deleted from that date. The war years saw drastic slowings, adding up to 3¼hr to the previous 8-8½hr scheduled and lengthening the trains from a maximum 10 vehicles to a regular loading of at least 14 cars. Acceleration followed in a very piecemeal fashion from 1945 onwards, but the

*Continued on page 39*

*Below:*
*Beauchief was the next station towards Midland after traffic from Manchester and Chesterfield had converged at Dore & Totley. This 1948 view was probably taken on a Sunday, as all running lines are signalled clear and there is not a trace of activity on the platforms.*

D. Thompson

*Above:*
*One of Grimesthorpe's allocation of Class 2 4-4-0s awaits departure southwards from Midland station on 4 May 1929.*
W. L. Good Collection

*Right:*
*At the time of opening in 1870, the new MR line northwards to Grimesthorpe was observed to pass through one of the dirtiest and smokiest parts of the town. The only station was located at Attercliffe Road, seen here amidst the smoke and gloom of a dull day in 1947.*
D. Thompson

*Right:*
*Only two intermediate stations were opened on the SDR, Catcliffe and Tinsley Road, and these were both closed to passenger traffic during September 1939. Catcliffe looks to be in a reasonable state in this 1947 view, with fire buckets and a seating bench still in place. Goods traffic lasted at the two stations until March 1955 and October 1960 respectively.*
D. Thompson

*Right*
*Coal trains did not make up the entire goods traffic scene on the ex-GCR line through Victoria. Class O4/1 2-8-0 No 3710 plods eastwards through Darnall West in the later 1940s with a train made up of assorted wooden-bodied vehicles.*
  B. R. Longbone Collection

*Right:*
*Shunting work at the collieries, steelworks and goods yards on the GCR system around Sheffield was the preserve of the Parker 0-6-2T engines for many years. The first of the class appeared in 1889 and the last was withdrawn in 1954, with most of the locomotives spending all their lives in the area. No 5623 is seen here shunting wagons at Neepsend in the mid-1930s, just west of the local power station*
  A.G.Ellis Collection

*Right:*
*The same location some 15 years later, with ex-ROD Class O4/3 No 63870 heading towards Woodhead with a freight on 27 June 1952. Pointwork into the loop and sidings has been altered and the spoil-heap in the background has become larger.*
  B. R. Goodlad

*Right:*
*Running powers from Manchester via Woodhead gave the London & North Western Railway access to the GCR at Victoria and thence to their own goods depots at City Goods and Bernard Road. LNWR 4-4-0 No 5354* New Zealand *is seen here during a pause at Beighton in the 1930s, alongside a colour-light signal which looks very modern compared to the ramshackle appearance of the 4-4-0*

A.G.Ellis Collection

*Right:*
*A far more dignified appearance is demonstrated by Class D9 4-4-0 No 6021* **Queen Mary**, *seen here at Victoria on 14 September 1929. Built in 1902 and named in April 1913, No 6021 was the penultimate member of the class to be withdrawn, as BR No 62307 in June 1950.*

W. L. Good

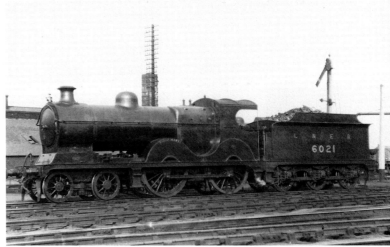

*Right:*
*After being displaced from express passenger work, the GNR Class C1 4-4-2s spent many years on secondary duties at various LNER depots. Mexborough had a small allocation, and the 'Klondykes' were well-liked locomotives which performed extremely well on duties between Sheffield, Doncaster and Hull. No 3254 is seen on the Victoria turntable on 14 September 1929.*

W. L. Good

*Right:*

*In early LNER days Neepsend and Mexborough had allocations of 12 and six Class C13 4-4-2 tank locomotives respectively for use on local passenger services, principally to Barnsley, Nottingham and Doncaster. Several of the class worked out their days in the area until withdrawal in the mid-1950s. No 6063, which survived as BR No 67408 until May 1954, is seen here at Neepsend loco.*

B. R. Longbone Collection

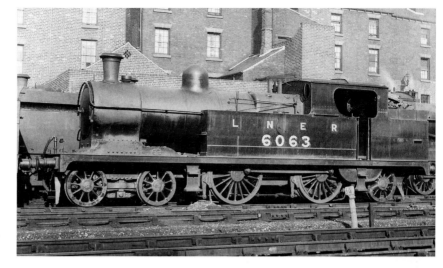

*Right:*

*Ex-North Eastern Railway Class S1 4-6-0 No 2115 awaits departure from Victoria with a special, probably Hull-bound, in the mid-1920s. These powerful and handsome locomotives had a relatively short life of less than 30 years' use, and often worked into Sheffield during their later years.*

B. R. Longbone Collection

*Right:*

*Robinson's six inside-cylindered 4-6-0s of 1912/13 were less than successful on main line express work due to poor steaming and a tendency for the driving axleboxes to overheat. After the introduction of the 'Director' 4-4-0s the class spent the rest of their lives on secondary work, and No 5425* City of Manchester *is seen here taking water at Victoria on 15 September 1930.*

W. L. Good

*Right:*
*The Class 9P 4-6-0s of 1917-20 were powerful machines which enjoyed a slightly better reputation than the earlier design, but they consumed coal at a voracious rate and became early targets for rebuilding in an attempt to curb their appetites. No 6166* Earl Haig *was fitted with Caprotti valve gear in 1929, which did reduce consumption considerably. In 1943 the locomotive was rebuilt again and emerged virtually as a Thompson 'B1' 4-6-0, but this was not successful and the loco was withdrawn in April 1949.*
D. Jackson Collection

*Right:*
*A Johnson Class 2 0-6-0 No 22970, seen at Brightside on 2 May 1949. The class dated back to 1875, but the rebuilt variety — as shown here, with Belpaire firebox — dated from 1917. A total of 865 were eventually built, and the last 30 survived well into the 1960s.*
A. G. Ellis Collection

*Right:*
*A peaceful scene at Dore & Totley station in 1948 as an LMS Class 5 4-6-0 pauses with a stopping train towards Derby. The Manchester lines are directly below the photographer, and a very simple form of catch-point is visible on the westbound line.*
D. Thompson

*Above:*
*Stanier-designed 'Jubilee'*
*No 5667* Jellicoe *is seen at*
*Sheffield Midland with a*
*northbound service.*
Real Photos/
Ian Allan Library

motive power which was available prevented any great
improvements taking place until 1954, when Class 6 or 7 power was
regularly rostered. Matters worsened in 1967 when the train was
diverted to run over the ex-Swinton & Knottingley route between
Sheffield and Leeds, and the subsidence-ridden trackwork kept the
schedule down to 71min, compared with a 1939 figure of 48min!
Just as the 'Waverley' could not possibly compete with the East
Coast main line for fast traffic to Edinburgh, neither could the
'Thames-Clyde Express' hope to survive in the face of London-
Glasgow electrification, and the title and service disappeared at the
end of the 1974-75 timetable. The essence of both trains was the
long-distance service they provided through the spine of England,
serving many large towns and cities en route from London to
Glasgow or Edinburgh. During their last years BR was not too
interested in providing such a service, and the post-Beeching era
was dominated more by route closures than by broadening the
services. Both trains fell victims to enforced cuts on the altars of
speed and utilisation.

*Above:*
The 'Devonian' in LMS days. Class 5 4-6-0 No 5096 hauls the southbound train through Millhouses & Ecclesall station, displaying a good collection of GWR coaching stock.
A. G. Ellis Collection

*Right:*
In 1932 the LMS introduced a class of 10 0-4-4Ts, Nos 6400-09. Although built under Stanier's auspices, the designs owed much to his predecessor, Fowler, and had been authorised in 1931. The locomotives were renumbered 1900-09 following the introduction of Ivatt's 2-6-0s in 1946. One of the class, No 6404, is pictured here.
L&GRP/
Ian Allan Library

*Bottom right:*
Another classic ex-Great Central design is seen at Neepsend in 1931. Robinson-designed Class D9 4-4-0 No 6026 was one of a class introduced in 1901.
L&GRP/
Ian Allan Library

The last of these trains, the 'Devonian', turned out to be the best survivor of the trio. In 1927 only three carriages went through from Bradford to Torquay and Paignton, the remainder of the train terminating at Bristol. Running along the LMSR was brisk, especially between Birmingham and Bristol, but the three onward coaches abandoned to the GWR then had a very leisurely amble on to South Devon. In these early days the southbound train paused at Sheffield for five minutes from 11.42am, with the return service arriving at 4.25pm. The train was certainly a prestigious working, especially after being accelerated in 1937 to give the fastest Leeds-Bristol time of 280min for the 206 miles. 'Jubilee' power gave the necessary speed, and in the summer months the entire train, including restaurant cars, worked between Bradford and Kingswear. The train disappeared in the war years but was reinstated in October 1946 as far as Torquay on slightly longer schedules of 8³/₄hr from Bradford and 8hr 57min return. Kingswear was reached again during the next year, but the services were slowed to 9hr 48min and 9hr 37min respectively and in winter the train operated unnamed between Bradford and Bristol.

The 'Devonian' then became a relentless survivor, taking in changes of routes, timings and motive power right up to the present time. The northern start was switched to Bradford (Exchange) station when the route was switched to the ex-S&K line in 1967, running throughout the year on a good schedule to Paignton. 'Peak' diesels were long associated with the rain, which carried restaurant cars and gave a rapid cross-country service from the West Riding to Torbay. The title disappeared in 1975, but the establishment of the full HST service on the northeast-southwest routes by 1982 heralded an eventual revival of the well-known name.

It was not until the summer of 1987 that the title was given to the existing Bradford-Paignton service, now reduced to 6hr 40min. Happily, the title is still with us in 1993, adorning the timetable pages of the 08.15 Leeds-Paignton and 08.33 Paignton-Newcastle return.

Capital expenditure during the late 1920s and early 1930s was minimal, with the trade depression giving thin times all round. Woodhouse loops were extended and an up line loop was laid in between Darnall and Woodburn, Victoria station gained a platform and Bridgehouses goods depot was slightly enlarged, and the yards at Roundwood and Woodhouse Mill were given extra wagon capacity. The LMSR laid now empty stock sidings at Heeley, Nunnery and Dore & Totley, and carried out some improvements at Queens Road goods depot.

What did happen during the 1930s was the commencement of the Manchester-Sheffield/Wath electrification scheme. The idea had first been considered in pre-1914 days, when the climbs to Woodhead were seeing endless processions of coal trains with a passenger service fitted in between. War and depression had delayed the scheme, but by the mid-1930s, with business picking up again, the existing trackwork could not be modified any further to take more traffic. Electrification had been successfully applied to mineral lines in the northeast during NER days, where heavy trains were operated by fewer locomotives on schedules far improved from steam-powered days. On any mixed goods/express passenger line the greatest benefits lay in better utilisation of track space and motive power, but on the Manchester line the state of the Woodhead tunnels added another dimension. Almost a century of incessant steam operation had rotted and blasted the twin single-line bores into decrepitude, and the elimination of steam power would prolong the remaining life of the tunnels.

Approval was given during October 1936 for a scheme requiring 88 new electric locomotives to replace 181 steam locos. It is interesting to compare the initial specification for the locomotive fleet with what finally emerged over 15 years later. Nine express passenger locos were ordered (seven were built), 69 mixed traffic locos (58 built) and ten banking locomotives were requested (none built). Eventually some of the ex-NER locomotives were rebuilt for use on the scheme, but these were quickly scrapped in favour of using the new mixed traffic machines — if not steam power — on the Worsborough incline out of Barnsley towards Penistone. Great things were hoped for, including express timings from Manchester being reduced from 55min to 46$\frac{1}{2}$min and average goods and mineral train speeds being increased by about half. Steam haulage would still be needed east of Victoria, and the changeover points were to be at Bernard Road and Woodhouse for the goods and mineral traffic. A new steam/diesel depot was laid out for the Darnall area to replace the ancient ex-MSLR Neepsend shed. Work went ahead rapidly and a completion date of late 1940 for all work except the locomotives and the new depot was within sight when the war stopped nearly all progress. Darnall new shed opened in 1943 and Neepsend survived as a depot of various sorts until demolition in the 1960s. Another casualty of wartime was the passenger service on the ex-District Railway, which had fallen to three trains each way between Sheffield and Mansfield when cancellation took place on 11 September 1939. At this level the service was bound to succumb, war or no war, but the ex-SDR route had a future which then lay some 25 years ahead.

*Right:*
*Thompson's first Class L1 2-6-4T engine appeared in May 1945 and was comprehensively tested over several parts of the LNER system. No 9000 is seen at Victoria station sometime before June 1946, when she was repainted in full LNER livery.*
A. G. Ellis Collection

PLATFORM
2W

**CHAPTER 4**

# The Postwar Years

T he electrification scheme was not revived until September 1947, by which time it had become clear that the Woodhead tunnels were almost beyond repair and could not possibly be used in their existing condition. Options were examined and a decision was made to cut a brand new double-track tunnel which would be concrete-lined and free of ventilation shafts — steam traction was not to be worked within the portals. Electric haulage started firstly between Wath and Dunford Bridge in February 1952, followed by the Manchester-Woodhead section in June 1954. A partial collapse within the new tunnel delayed the full opening until September of that year, and the new electric services took full effect with the winter timetable starting on the 20th of the month. Delays with installing new signalling equipment eastwards from Victoria held up the completion of the last phase, to Rotherwood, until February 1955. A new turntable was built here for turning steam locomotives after arrival from the South Yorkshire/East Midlands coalfields, and beyond this date all steam haulage to Penistone officially ceased.

The early postwar period saw the introduction of the 'Master Cutler', perhaps Sheffield's most famous named passenger service and one which survives today after two route changes and several modes of haulage. The prewar Marylebone breakfast car special was revived, with an extra stop at Rugby inserted, on a 3hr 50min schedule which was cut back to 3hr 35min and given the new title from October 1947. The train was well-filled, but had difficulty keeping good time until the new 'B1' 4-6-0s were replaced by Gresley's ex-LNER 'A3' 4-6-2s in 1951. By 1958 the title had disappeared from the ex-GCR route and was transferred to a new diesel-hauled 7.20am Pullman departure for King's Cross via Retford, giving a 2hr 45min service to the capital. The Pullman set worked a return Sheffield journey during the day before returning as the down 'Master Cutler' from King's Cross at 7.20pm. Success quickly followed, with passengers actually being turned away during the first few weeks of operation, and a regular healthy loading was established.

During the later 1960s BR had one of their corporate brainstorms and decided that future 'policy' would dictate all Sheffield-London traffic being concentrated on the Midland main line, hence the 'Cutler' could not be allowed to continue in its present successful form! The four Pullman services disappeared, and the train sets were used on a new 'Hull Pullman' service. The 'Master Cutler' title was given to a non-Pullman Midland line departure at 7.15am which gave a 2hr 43min service, and 2hr 30min was eventually achieved during 1972. Ten years later HST haulage brought the time down to 2hr 18min. The title survives today, gracing the timetable pages of the 0720 departure from Sheffield and return from St Pancras at 1700, giving journeys of 2hr 10min and 2hr 11min respectively.

A much shorter-lived train was the 'South Yorkshireman', another prewar revival routed via the ex-GCR route which led a rather patchy existence. The main train left Victoria at 11.27am after

*Previous page:*
*The Newcastle-Bournemouth service arrives at Victoria behind York-based 'B16/3' No 61464 on 15 July 1958. The train reversed at Sheffield and was taken forward at 12.2pm. Notice the early BR dark blue enamel signs, the loco crews in conversation and the covered walkway giving direct access to the Victoria Hotel.*
*J. H. Turner*

having a portion from Bradford and Huddersfield attached, and eventually reached Marylebone at 3.30pm. The return working left London at 4.44pm and reached Sheffield by 8.42pm, but both trains ran rather empty and during a coal shortage in 1951 they were cancelled for several weeks. The run-down of ex-GCR line services continued throughout the 1950s and culminated in the withdrawal of through passenger services north of Nottingham in 1960, when the 'South Yorkshireman' disappeared.

The British Railways Modernisation Plan of 1955 had great changes in store for Sheffield's motive power depots. Grimesthorpe, Millhouses and Darnall were all to be swept away, together with their locomotives, and replaced by a new diesel depot built at Tinsley. Grimesthorpe dated from the early 1860s and boasted extensive workshop facilities by the turn of the century. Improved coal and ash handling equipment was installed by the LMSR during 1937, and in 1958 the depot received its final code of 41B when the Eastern Region took over the entire Sheffield area. Closure took place officially from December 1961, but the site was used as a diesel loco stabling point during 1962 until demolition took place at the end of the year to make way for a new freight depot.

Millhouses shed was opened in 1901 and was at first called Ecclesall, a sub-shed to Grimesthorpe. Passenger locomotives were supplied from Millhouses, (with Grimesthrope supplying the goods and mixed traffic power), and during MR and early LMSR days the fleet was predominantly made up of 4-4-0 classes. 'Jubilee' 4-6-0s arrived later, but the Eastern Region quickly began to reduce the fleet to scrap after the 1958 takeover. Closure took place on 1 January 1962.

Work resumed on the electric depot at Darnall after 1945, but it was not completed until 1952, alongside the rest of the MSW scheme. Even then, the depot was used for only eight years until the first members of the new diesel fleet arrived at Darnall and displaced the 1,500V dc machines to Reddish (Manchester) and Wath. Darnall shed had a very short life of only 20 years, but some very interesting locomotives were to be found there. As well as housing a good spread of LNER classes from 'B1' 4-6-0s and 'V2' 2-6-2s to 'O1' 2-8-0s and 'L1' 2-6-4Ts, several venerable ex-GCR survivors ended their days at the depot in the late 1940s such as the 'B7' 4-6-0s and several of the original Class D10 'Director' 4-4-0s. Even the surviving 'B8' 'Glenalmond' 4-6-0s put in an appearance before the difficulties of carrying out successions of repairs finally saw the last examples consigned for scrap. After closure in June 1963 the site was used for wagon repair duties until the mid-1980s, but today the area has been abandoned to dereliction and decay.

The greatest changes produced by the 1958 reorganisation were the building of the new Tinsley marshalling yard and adjacent motive power depot. Sheffield's abundance of small goods yards and MPDs was to be replaced by one yard, one diesel depot and a single freight terminal on the site of Brightside loco shed. Wagon repair work was intended to be done at a planned new shop to be built at Woodhouse Mill, but later economies saw this work moved to the closed shed at Darnall.

By the early 1960s the former District Railway was virtually unused, but the route was chosen to provide sites for the new marshalling yard and diesel depot because of the availability of land and due to the good access which could easily be provided at both ends of the layout. Work started in 1961, and, just as had happened 65 years previously, a large amount of civil engineering work was needed. Two years later a new north-facing curve at Treeton was completed, and the last new connection was completed at Shepcote Lane during the summer of 1964. The diesel depot opened in February 1964, ending what must have been a difficult year of maintenance work at Darnall. Official opening of the entire scheme took place on 29 October 1966. Grimesthorpe Freight Terminal opened in summer 1965, and the demise of the city's good yards followed in the next 12 months. The remains of Sheffield's earliest monument to the railway age, at Wicker Goods Yard, were destroyed by fire in July 1966.

The last years of steam operation provided one or two highlights to relieve the gloom being spread by the ever-pervading diesel fleet. During the 1957-60 period the surviving Class D11 'Improved Director' 4-4-0s were used from Darnall during the summer timetables for excursion and ECS work, and the new BR Standard '9F' 2-10-0s displayed their great abilities for passenger work on several duties in the area. These were, however, merely short breaks in a generally cloudy picture, and the area's remaining steam power was shuffled across to Canklow depot, near Rotherham, until closure here took place in October 1965. A few visiting locos could be seen beyond this time, but only until September 1966 when all remaining facilities were withdrawn.

*Below:*
*After closure as a locomotive shed in 1943, Neepsend survived as a wagon depot until demolition in the mid-1960s. This view shows three unfitted wagons and a Belgian ferry van at the depot shortly before closure.*
*J. H. Turner*

*Right:*
*Some interesting point - and crossing - work can be seen in this view of Class EM1 No 26037 entering Victoria from the west in September 1961.*
B. Haresnape

*Right:*
*Stanier Class 3 2-6-2T No 40181 enters Rotherham (Masborough) station with the 'Barnsley Flyer', a Sheffield (Midland)-Rotherham-Cudworth-Barnsley local working in early BR days.*
Ian Allan Library

*Right:*
*A wet and gloomy scene at the east end of Victoria station on 12 April 1951. Class C13 4-4-2T No 67411 departs with an ECS train made up of former GCR stock, whilst Class O4/3 No 63840 waits at the platform starter signal. No 63840 was rebuilt to Class O4/8 in August 1957.*
A. G. Ellis Collection

*Right:*
Another scene at the east end of Victoria, showing rebuilt 'B16/3' 4-6-0 No 61476 arriving with a York-Bournemouth train in the 1950s. The locomotive received the full Thompson rebuilding treatment in June 1945 after 25 years in her NER glory, and the coaching stock is made up of LNER/BR vehicles instead of the SR stock which also worked this service.
A. G. Ellis Collection

*Right:*
Being closely observed by two young spotters is Class D11 4-4-0 No 62662 Prince of Wales *backing out of Victoria en route to Darnall shed on 25 July 1959. Notice how some of the smokebox fittings have been picked out in white paint, and also the lower position of the cabside number which always distinguished this particular locomotive. Alongside is one of the comparatively ugly LMS 'Flying Pig' 2-6-0s Nos 43058, prior to working a Nottingham local. On the extreme right an ex-Tweedmouth 'V2' 2-6-2 No 60808 waits for a southbound express to Marylebone, whilst an 'O4' 2-8-0 approaches with a down freight. A truly busy scene!*
J. H. Turner

*Right:*
Always regarded as handsome engines, although rough riding according to many drivers, 'Sandringham' 'B17' 4-6-0 No 61643 Champion Lodge *of March shed makes a good start from Victoria with the Liverpool-Harwich boat train on 6 April 1957. The exhaust may not have been appreciated by passengers and railway staff, but it was very acceptable for the photographer.*
J. H. Turner

*Right:*
'Jubilee' Class 4-6-0 No 45590 *Travancore forges up the 1 in 100 through Dore & Totley station on 3 October 1959 with the 10.30am Bradford (Forster Square)-St Pancras station.*
M. Mensing

*Below:*
Immingham Class K3 No 61966 *is seen here about to leave Woodhouse East sidings with a Saturdays only ECS working to Grimsby on 13 January 1951. The signal gantry has a good collection of GCR posts and finials, and the sidings alongside the train contain two two-car Cravens DMUs (Nos M51681/M51706 and M51682/M51707) awaiting delivery to Newton Heath, Manchester. The Cravens factory was turning out a steady stream of DMUs at the time, and siding space at Darnall was often insufficient.*
J. H. Turner

**50**

*Right:*
*Another scene at Broughton Lane, looking towards Rotherham and showing Class O4/8 2-8-0 No 63882 giving assistance to a Sheffield-bound freight train.*
B. R. Longbone Collection

*Right:*
*Rotherham Central was renamed Rotherham & Masboro' from January 1889, but reverted to the original form from September 1950. Closure to passengers took place on 5 September 1966 — the blackest day for all ex-GCR stations — and to goods traffic from May 1968. Class 31 No 31278 trundles a string of mineral empties northwards through the site on 21 March 1977.*
K. Lane

*Right:*
*Rotherham Road Sidings lay just to the north of Central station, well situated for steelworks traffic. Class 20s Nos 20022 and 20032 start a mixed freight out of the sidings en route to Rawmarsh on 24 July 1975.*
P. D. Hawkins

*Right:*
*Despite having taken over 30 years to achieve, the opening of the direct route from Sheffield to Chesterfield was done without any ceremony at all. The steep descent into the city from Bradway tunnel had always been over-estimated in terms of operating difficulties, and this view shows Compound 4-4-0s Nos 41053 and 41003 descending towards Dore & Totley station with a Derby-Sheffield local on 16 June 1951.*

B. R. Goodlad

*Right:*
*The lack of activity in this September 1964 scene at Millhouses & Ecclesall is probably symptomatic of the general decline of railway business which had taken place in recent years. The motive power depot can be seen behind the line of empty coaching stock.*

D. Thompson

*Right:*
*Class 4F 0-6-0 No 44267 starts the climb out to Heeley Carriage Sidings with the stock from an excursion working which has been terminated at Midland station on 4 August 1956. On the extreme left can be seen the end of the burrowing junction built as part of the 1900 alterations.*

B. R. Goodlad

**52**

*Right:*
*Snowplough-fitted Class 5*
*4-6-0 No 45120 leaves via the*
*centre road with an ECS*
*train towards Heeley on*
*12 April 1963. Modern*
*concrete flats have replaced*
*terraced housing in the*
*background.*
G. T. Robinson

*Right:*
*At Beighton the new GCR*
*line towards Nottingham and*
*London passed directly above*
*the MR 'Old Road' by means*
*of a lattice girder bridge.*
*Austerity 2-8-0 No 90153*
*heads south along the route*
*towards Killamarsh with a*
*goods train on 24 May 1955.*
B. R. Goodlad

*Right:*
*The same bridge, this time*
*viewed from alongside the*
*MR line as Stanier '8F' 2-8-0*
*No 48306 heads south with a*
*coal train on 14 August 1954.*
B. R. Goodlad

*Right:*
Another scene of a southbound goods on the 'Old Road' at Beighton, this time being hauled by ex-LMSR 0-6-0 No 43863 on 12 September 1953. BR's remaining freight traffic today seems to be made up almost entirely of monotonous merry-go-round or tanker trains - the almost bewildering collection of stock behind the Class 4F's tender could now only be seen as a special attraction on a preserved railway. This scene would be largely swept away over the following 10 years.

B. R. Goodlad

*Right:*
Power output may not have been a strong point for many former Midland Railway locomotives, but longevity was a feature of many Derby products. Johnson Class 3F 0-6-0 No 43605 was approaching 70 years of life when photographed coming down the Kiveton Park colliery branch with the daily freight on 19 June 1954. An ex-GCR 'Pom-Pom' 0-6-0 can be seen stood on the main line near Killamarsh Junction, just above the train.

B. R. Goodlad

*Right:*
One of Darnall shed's Class O4/1 2-8-0s, No 63783, approaches Woodhouse East Junction from the Retford line with a train of wagons on 29 August 1959. The two wooden-bodied wagons are piled high with scrap steel, probably destined for the steelworks. To the left of the loco the MR 'Old Road' can just be discerned in the distance.

J. H. Turner

*Right:*
*Photographed on 4 October 1952 and still carrying her LMS number, Johnson 0-4-4T No 1370 pauses between pilot duties at Midland station.*

B. R. Goodlad

*Right:*
*Another view of a rebuilt Johnson Class 2 0-6-0, showing No 58209 on Millhouses shed on 27 May 1951.*

W. L. Good

*Right:*
*Like many other British locomotive manufacturers, the Yorkshire Engine Co sent its products far and wide over a long period, but this view shows two locomotives destined for use quite near home. GWR Hawksworth-designed 0-6-0PTs Nos 8466 and 8467 are seen near completion at the Meadowhall works on 13 January 1951. This small works built no less than 30 of these sturdy-looking locos for the Western Region of BR, and like so many classes which were constructed after 1945, they had an all-too-short life.*

J. H. Turner

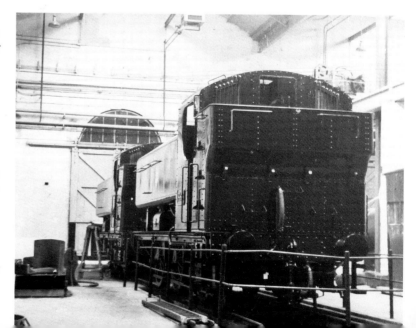

*Right:*
BR Standard Class 5 4-6-0
No 73000 pauses at
Millhouses & Ecclesall with
a Sheffield-Derby slow train
in September 1958.
          Ian Allan Library

*Right:*
Birmingham (Saltley) shed's
Class 5 No 44966 forges
uphill past Beauchief
carriage sidings with a
Bristol express on 4 April
1954. Notice the
immaculately-trimmed
ballast and the clearly visible
gradient of the main line
compared to the carriage
siding trackwork.
          B. R. Goodlad

*Right:*
4 July 1953 must have been
a hot summer's day — the
signalman at Dore & Totley
West Junction has opened
every possible window to
obtain some ventilation
within his grimy cabin! Ex-
LMS Compound 4-4-0
No 41154 passes by with the
4.46pm stopper to
Manchester.
          B. R. Goodlad

**56**

*Right:*
*Two scenes just south of Midland station on 16 July 1955. The first shows another ex-LMS Compound 4-4-0, No 41071, departing with a Manchester stopping train and passing the railway offices known as the 'Kremlin' to the rear. This compound loco bears several differences to No 41154 shown in the previous photograph.*
B. R. Goodlad

*Right:*
*A little later in the day sees Caprotti-fitted Class 5 4-6-0 No 44754 passing the same spot with a Newcastle-Bristol express. The train is on the up Chesterfield line, and the down line can be seen emerging from the burrowing junction on the left. The centre roads are for Manchester traffic — as witnessed by the previous scene of No 41071 — and the whole layout is very much as left after the quadrupling of 1900.*
B. R. Goodlad

*Right:*
*With a clean exhaust and barely a leak in sight, Class 5 4-6-0 No 44828 departs from Midland with a relief to the up 'Thames-Clyde Express' on 30 July 1955.*
B. R. Goodlad

*Right:*
*A one-time classic combination of motive power on the Midland main line! An LMS-built 4-4-0, No 40581, pilots an unidentified 'Jubilee' 4-6-0 on the down 'Waverley' into Midland station in August 1958. At Leeds the two locos would be replaced with a Holbeck 'Scot' or 'Jubilee' for the journey via the Settle and Carlisle and thence via the Waverley route to Edinburgh. One wonders how many of the passengers would appreciate the motive power and the magnificent scenery en route?*
                    J. H. Turner

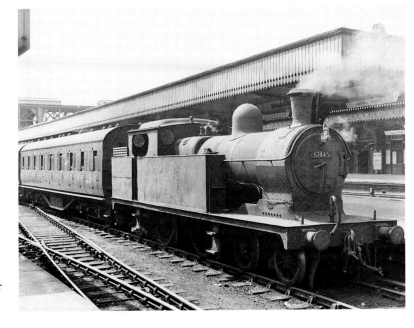

*Right:*
*A Great Central interloper in Midland station! Robinson 'C14' 4-4-2T No 67445 (from Barnsley GC shed) is seen about to depart with a local train to Barnsley Court House station on 9 May 1959. Nos 67445, 67447 and 67448 were transferred from Gorton to Barnsley in the late 1950s, from where they worked the Penistone-Barnsley-Doncaster service for a short time. It was unusual to find one in Midland station, and all were withdrawn by the end of 1959.*
                    J. H. Turner

*Right:*
*Another visitor to Victoria from far-off places. Southern Railway Bulleid Pacific No 34006 Bude takes part in the 1948 locomotive exchange trials, for which purpose a Stanier tender has been fitted to ensure adequate water capacity.*
                    A. G. Ellis Collection

**58**

*Right:*
*Thompson 'B1' 4-6-0*
*No 61151 approaches*
*Victoria near Woodburn*
*Junction with a Hull-*
*Liverpool express on 11 April*
*1952. The poor quality of coal*
*on the tender is typical of the*
*period; shortages led to*
*several cancellations at this*
*time.*
    A. G. Ellis Collection

*Centre right:*
*Gresley Class A3 No 60102*
**Sir Frederick Banbury**
*awaits the up 'South*
*Yorkshireman' at Victoria*
*station in the early 1950s.*
*This locomotive was the*
*second GNR 4-6-2 to be*
*built, in July 1922, and was a*
*regular GCR section*
*performer in the early 1950s..*
    A. G. Ellis Collection

*Below right:*
*A total of 58 Robinson 'O4'*
*2-8-0s were rebuilt from 1944*
*to 1949 with 'B1'-type boilers*
*and cylinders and*
*Walschaerts valve gear, but*
*keeping the original pony*
*truck in the interests of*
*economy. Many other 'O4s'*
*which had good cylinders and*
*valve gear were rebuilt with*
*just a new boiler, becoming*
*class 'O4/8'. Fully rebuilt*
*Class O1 No 63863 passes*
*Darnall West on an early*
*1950s goods working.*
    B. R. Longbone Collection

*Opposite page-bottom:*
*Taken from a little further to*
*the south and looking in the*
*opposite direction compared*
*with the previous*
*photograph, Class K3/2*
*No 61839 is seen storming*
*up the last few yards of 1 in*
*130 from Waleswood onto the*
*main line at Killamarsh. The*
*train is an up fish working*
*from Grimsby, and the date is*
*9 October 1956.*
    B. R. Goodlad

*Right:*
One can almost hear the syncopated three-cylinder beat of Class V2 2-6-2 No 60831 as she passes over the Midland main line near Killamarsh with the 3.20pm Marylebone-Manchester express on 17 June 1959. The train would be handed over to electric haulage, using a class EM2 Co-Co machine, at Victoria.

C. W. Woodhead

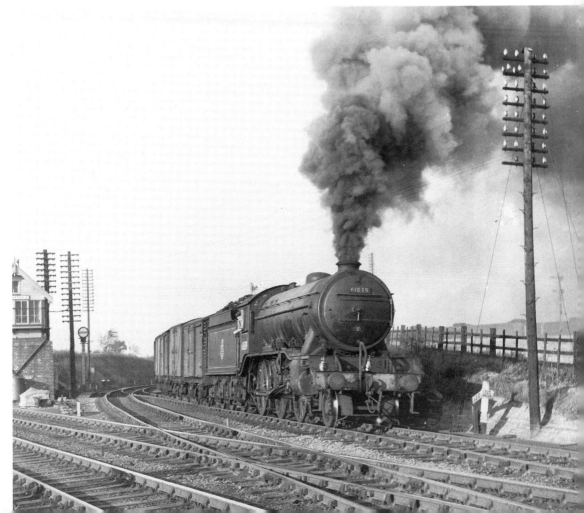

*Right:*
*The Gresley/Metropolitan Vickers Class EM1 Bo-Bo electric locomotives would rarely win any prizes for attractive appearance, but they excelled in the task for which they were produced — hauling heavy coal trains over Woodhead and giving greatly improved line capacity compared with steam traction. No 26015 passes through Victoria with a block load of coal from Westthorpe Colliery to Clarence Dock power station, Liverpool, on 3 July 1959.*
P. J. Lynch

*Below:*
*Coal haulage in pre-mgr days. Class EM1 No 26056* **Triton** *descends into Victoria with an up train empties on 22 July 1963. At least one wooden-bodied wagon is visible.* B. Stephenson

*Right:*
*The trackwork at Victoria station, showing the alterations made at the west end during 1953 when the No 3 signalbox was enlarged and rebuilt to supervise the improved layout.*

S. R. Batty

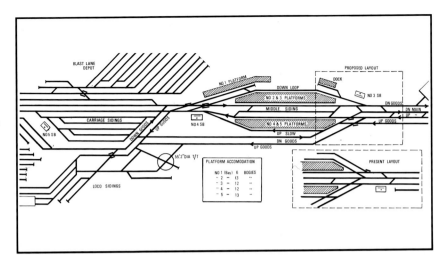

*Right:*
*The reception lines and express freight yard at Tinsley were equiped with 1,500V dc overhead supplies, and the insulation was capable of allowing a rapid conversion to 6.25kV or 25kV ac power if needed. No26049 Jason passes Tinsley Park box on departure from the main yard.*

British Railways

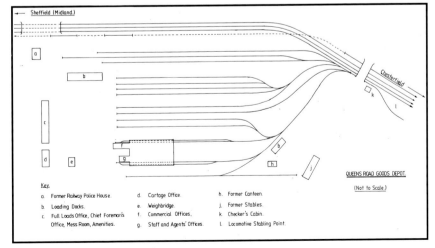

*Right:*
*Queens Roads Goods Depot, 1950.*

S. R. Batty

Key.

a. Former Railway Police House.
b. Loading Docks.
c. Full Loads Office, Chief Foreman's Office, Mess Room, Amenities.
d. Cartage Office.
e. Weighbridge.
f. Commercial Offices,
g. Staff and Agents' Offices.
h. Former Canteen.
j. Former Stables.
k. Checker's Cabin.
l. Locomotive Stabling Point.

QUEENS ROAD GOODS DEPOT.
(Not to Scale)

*Above:*
*Only seven locomotives were built purely for the haulage of passenger trains. The Class EM2 Co-Co machines were powerful 2,490hp locos which had a somewhat more attractive appearance than their freight-traffic cousins. No 27000* Electra *emerges from Thurgoland tunnel with a Penistone-Sheffield local in the 1950s.*

K. Field

*Above right:*
*Wicker Goods Depot, 1950.*

S. R. Batty

*Right:*
*Train No 1E14 being worked into Sheffield (Midland) by diesel shunter No 3336 after the train locomotive (Class 46 No 192) had caught fire on 29 September 1970. The use of diesel shunters with loaded passenger trains was by no means uncommon as Sheffield was the point at which the separate sections of northeast/southwest trains were combined prior to heading south over the Midland main line.*

Dr L. A. Nixon

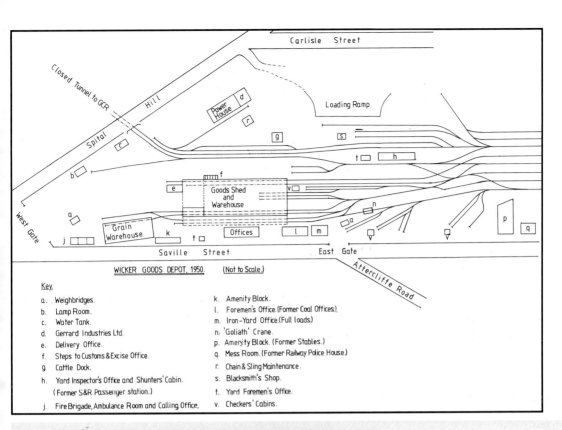

Carlisle Street

Closed Tunnel to GCR

Spital Hill

West Gate

Power House

Loading Ramp

Goods Shed and Warehouse

Grain Warehouse

Offices

Saville Street

East Gate

Attercliffe Road

WICKER GOODS DEPOT, 1950.    (Not to Scale.)

Key.

a. Weighbridges.
b. Lamp Room.
c. Water Tank.
d. Gerrard Industries Ltd.
e. Delivery Office.
f. Steps to Customs & Excise Office.
g. Cattle Dock.
h. Yard Inspector's Office and Shunters' Cabin.
   (Former S&R Passenger station.)
j. Fire Brigade, Ambulance Room and Calling Office.

k. Amenity Block.
l. Foremen's Office. (Former Coal Offices.)
m. Iron-Yard Office. (Full loads.)
n. 'Goliath' Crane.
p. Amenity Block. (Former Stables.)
q. Mess Room. (Former Railway Police House.)
r. Chain & Sling Maintenance.
s. Blacksmith's Shop.
t. Yard Foremen's Office.
v. Checkers' Cabins.

*Right:*
*Rail-blue liveried No 27006*
*Pandora draws into*
*Victoria with stock for the*
*16.50 to Manchester on*
*30 August 1966*
R.B.Partridge

*Right:*
*The dreaded blue and yellow*
*paints blighted all that*
*moved during the late 1960s.*
*Class EM1 No E26044*
*starts the climb out of*
*Victoria with a westbound*
*coal train on 14 June 1968.*
V. Bamford

*Right:*
*The layout at Sheffield*
*(Midland) station in 1953.*

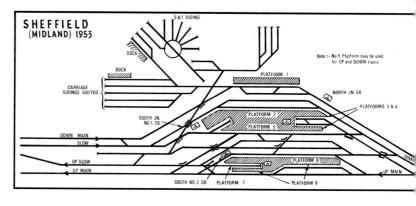

*Above:*
*A stranger in the camp —*
*Bristol-based 'Patriot' 4-6-0*
*No 45504* Royal Signals
*arrives at Victoria with the*
*diverted 10.30am Bristol-*
*Newcastle train on*
*27 November 1959. Several*
*trains were diverted on this*
*occasion through Victoria*
*due to the District*
*Engineers' possession of the*
*Midland main line at*
*Sheepbridge to excavate a fire*
*in the embankment.*
        C. W. Woodhead

*Right:*
*Passenger services*
*withdrawal notice as*
*discovered amongst the*
*rubbish on Victoria's*
*platform five, over eight*
*years after closure.*

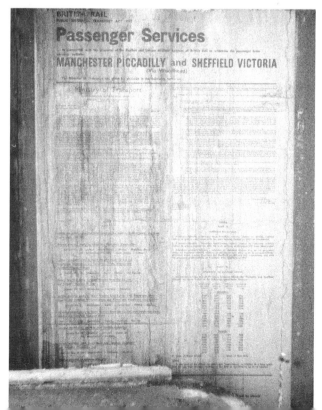

*Right:*
*Bridgehouses Goods Depot,*
*1950.*

S. R. Batty

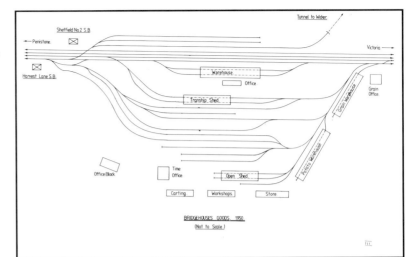

*Below:*
*Morning sunshine graces the*
*09.23 arrival at Victoria of*
*E26055* Prometheus *with*
*an early train from*
*Manchester on 23 October*
*1969.*

V. Bamford

*Right:*
*A small gathering witnessed the arrival at Victoria of E26054* Pluto *with the 14.10 from Manchester on Saturday 3 January 1970, the last day of electrically-hauled passenger services.*

I.S.Carr

*Below:*
*E26034 passes the Cravens works at Darnall with a westbound coal train on 26 August 1971.*

T. Whitham

*Above:*
*Many of the 'EM1'*
*locomotives were equipped for*
*working in multiple for*
*haulage of merry-go-round*
*coal trains across the*
*Pennines during the 1970s.*
*Nos 76012 and 76027 are*
*seen leaving Orgreave Yard*
*with a coal train on 14 July*
*1977.*

N. E. Preedy

*Right:*
*Railways in Sheffield &*
*Rotherham.*

S. R. Batty

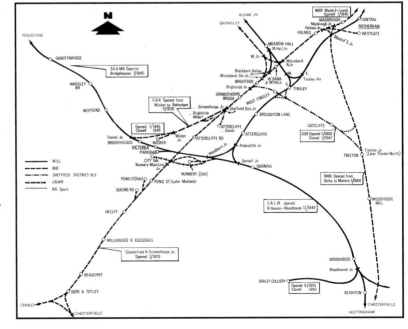

# CHAPTER 5

# Recent Developments

T he bulk of the Modernisation Plan work was completed by 1965, but the following five years saw more closures of stations in the area and the end of the ex-GCR line south to Nottingham and London. The improved Nunnery curve (from the north end of Midland station on to the Victoria-Retford/Nottingham lines just west of Woodburn junction) gave better access for reversal of passenger traffic between the two main-line stations. During 1965 much of Victoria's local traffic was diverted away to Midland station, and the writing was clearly on the wall for the city's electrified main line. The Manchester trains, the 'Continental' and the surviving cross-country services remained unaltered, but the end was brought nearer with the closure of the entire GCR line in September 1966. Closure proposals were published in late 1968 and the electrified passenger services ceased running on 5 January 1970. The freight traffic continued, but only until this too became an alleged liability. Steel and coal traffic dwindled away; the old arguments about high renewal costs, expensive maintenance and lack of profitability were all wheeled out and eventually the Woodhead line was closed from July 1981. DMU services to Huddersfield continued to pass through the abandoned, decaying remains of Victoria on their way to or from Penistone, but these were later diverted to run via Barnsley and so complete the closure process.

Multiple-aspect signalling (MAS) work started as long ago as 1971, but 11 long years were to pass before the scheme was eventually completed. The quadruple track out to Dore & Totley was reduced to double track by the time the new power signalbox was opened in January 1973, and completion of Phase 1 was officially announced in June of that year when temporary panels at Dore & Totley and Brightside were finally removed. Mechanical signalboxes at Midland station, Heeley, Millhouses and Queens Road all disappeared. Phase 2 was completed in January 1979, and by that year's summer all boxes had vanished from Wincobank, Holmes, Canklow and Rotherham Masborough. The scheme was finally completed in late 1982 after extensive work at Treeton finally saw MAS applied to all ex-Midland lines in the area.

High Speed Trains arrived late in Sheffield, principally because the new sets were deployed on the lucrative East Coast, West of England and South Wales routes as they were delivered. The St Pancras service was not deemed to be worthwhile for such investment, and the era of the HST did not reach Sheffield until October 1981 when many of the northeast-southwest services (NE/SW) were turned over to the new traction. The recessionary forces of the early 1980s led to a revamping of BR's entire HST fleet diagrams, and enough sets were pruned from existing services — including the NE/SW route — to allow six trains to be allocated to the Midland main line from October 1982. Thus the 'Cutler' received a welcome boost in status if not speed, and the replacement of the Pullman stock seemed doomed to impossibility. Financial problems delayed the upgrading of the full Midland main line for years and killed off for good provisional plans to drastically

*Previous page:*
*Despite being built for freight purposes, Tinsley frequently hosted many locomotives regularly employed on passenger duties. 'Peak' Class 45 No 45004* Royal Irish Fusilier *takes refuge at the depot on 12 July 1981.*
M. J. Collins

*Continued on page 76*

*Right:*
*Heading for Midland station via reversal at Nunnery, a two-car DMU crosses the Wicker Arches and approaches the closed remains of Victoria station on 3 August 1978*
D. Pearce

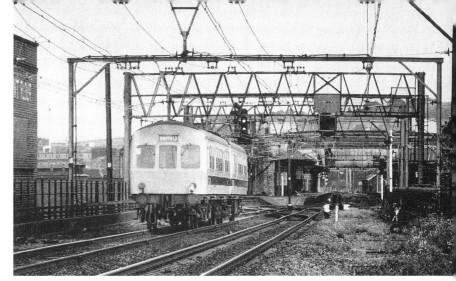

*Right:*
*Trackwork and signalling being reduced at Masborough Station South Junction on 17 August 1978.*
D. Pearce

*Right:*
*A slightly later view of the same location, with the same debris still in view. Class 31 No 31204 hauls the 08.15 Birmingham-Leeds service around the curve on a freezing, misty 1 December 1978.*
A. R. Kaye

*Right:*
*Masborough South Junction on 31 October 1977, with Class 20s Nos 20060 and 20034 stood on an up tippler train and Class 31 No 31316 approaching with a ballast working. The lines in the foreground are the west-to-south connection between the former S&RR and NMR lines.*

C. R. Davies.

*Right:*
*At the peak of the system's activity, sidings capacity in the Sheffield and Rotherham area was vital to ensure rapid handling of the steelworks traffic. Masborough Sorting Sidings are long abandoned in this view of Class 37 No 37039 passing with a freight destined for Tinsley Yard on 21 April 1978. The sidings in the left mid-distance were the site of the erstwhile Sheffield Freightliner base.*

T. Dodgson

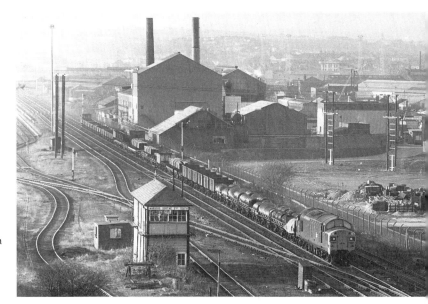

*Right:*
*Class 60 No 60005* Skiddaw *passes the site of Holmes station with a Peak Forest-Selby stone train on 11 May 1993.*

S. R. Batty

*Right:*
*Class 47 No 47616* The Red Dragon *passes the site of Wincobank station on 3 July 1989 with a 16-coach Scottish Land Cruise train returning to St Pancras. This location is now the site of Meadowhall station, and preliminary site work on the shopping centre appears to be underway in the background.*
A. Taylor

*Right:*
*Class 76 Bo-Bo electric locomotives Nos 76022 and 76023, displaying different BR symbols, approach Darnall West with a coal train on 28 May 1981, during the last few weeks of electric operation.*
D. C. Pearce

*Right:*
*Class 37s Nos 37019 and 37064 pass through Woodhouse station with a train of eastbound coal empties on 10 September 1981.*
C. J. Marsden

*Right:*
*Looking rather like a ghost from the slip-coach era, Class 153 No 153326 approaches Woodhouse station from the Retford direction on 19 March 1993. The greatly-reduced yard is clearly visible, and the background shows another common feature of the late 20th century industrial landscape — reclaimed spoilheaps.*
S. R. Batty

*Right*
*The recession of the early 1980s did tremendous damage to the steel industry, inflicting mortal blows which saw endless factories closed and levelled. Plenty of trackwork is still in use in this view taken on 2 June 1977, showing Class 20s Nos 20208 and 20133 passing Rotherham Road box with just a brake van in tow.*
G. W. Morrison

*Right:*
*Despite losing its regular passenger stopping services from the early 1950s until 1966, the ex-GCR Sheffield-Rotherham line has always been useful as a diversionary route when traffic has been unable to use the ex-MR Midland-Masborough line. Rebuilding work in connection with the Meadowhall Interchange alterations on 1 May 1989 saw a Sprinter DMU crossing the Don on the GCR route near Tinsley East Junction.*
A. Taylor

*Right:*
*HST power on the GCR. The 17.08 York-Plymouth approaches Tinsley East Junction whilst being diverted away from the MR route on 1 May 1989. After leaving the regular Doncaster-Sheffield line at Mexborough, the train will enter Midland station via Woodburn Junction and the Nunnery Curve.*
A. Taylor

*Right:*
*Looking towards Sheffield, a Sprinter DMU prepares to pass below the ex-NMR route between Tinsley and Rotherham with a diverted service on 1 May 1989.*
A. Taylor

*Right:*
*Class 40 No 40029 Saxonia makes a rousing start up the climb to Dore & Totley with the Cleethorpes-Manchester empty parcels vans on 3 August 1983. Evidence of track reduction can be clearly seen*
A. Taylor

improve the line northwards to Leeds via Wath Road and Normanton. Electrification to St Pancras was the ultimate goal — the idea had been around since the 1960s, and had made local airport plans since then totally unviable — but this scheme too eventually withered away.

The local government reorganisation of 1974 had led to the establishment of passenger transport authorities in many parts of the country. Each authority was given the responsibility of setting up the best local passenger transport system which the metropolitan areas could afford, and a great deal of research went into deciding which mix of road and rail transport would serve the area best. It wasn't just a case of integrating existing facilities — consideration of population locations, existing travelling habits, regular journeys for work and leisure, future land use plans and the availability (or otherwise) of hard cash all combined to produce the final picture. South Yorkshire emerged as a predominantly bus-based system, with a heavily-subsidised fares policy which gave ultra-cheap mass transport for Sheffield's travellers. The neighbouring West Yorkshire PTA swung heavily towards railway-based travel and made a name for itself with schemes involving the reopening of closed stations, building of new ones in heavily-populated areas and the upkeep of those which BR would otherwise have quickly closed. New rolling stock was built and new service patterns introduced to such effect that rail travel in the area boomed way beyond levels BR would never have dreamt of.

The two PTA areas had a long common boundary, but getting the South Yorkshire authority to co-operate in producing joint services was no easy task. The Leeds/Barnsley/Sheffield service was successful, but the Sheffield/Penistone/Huddersfield run was achieved only after considerable haggling over money had been got around. In a perfect world, this service would have been extended to reach Halifax and Bradford, but the costs involved in West Yorkshire ruled this out.

Eventually a start was made in improving some of the area's local railway services. Road traffic between Sheffield, Rotherham and Doncaster was at choking point, and the existing lines could be modified to provide a solution. Masborough station, although large and endowed with plenty of platform space, was seen as too far away from the town centre to be of much practical use. The ex-GCR Rotherham (Central) site was dilapidated but well-placed, and a start was made on building a new station here and also on a new connecting line from Holmes, on the ex-NMR route just south of Masborough, across to the ex-GCR line near the new station. The new line — the Holmes Chord — opened on 12 April 1987, followed by the new Central station on 11 May.

By this time another development was underway — the creation of a massive shopping centre at Meadowhall, close by the conglomeration of ex-NMR/SYR lines in the Meadowhall/Wincobank area and the junction of the lines from Barnsley and Leeds. The entire area was blighted by decay and dereliction, and the plans for the shopping centre were aimed at showing exactly what could be done to regenerate such an area. A new railway station was essential, and accordingly plans were made for Meadowhall station to be built at the junction of the Leeds and Barnsley lines, just north of the existing Brightside station. Opening took place on 5 September 1990, placing the centre within minutes of Sheffield and Rotherham and providing good access from Leeds, Barnsley and Doncaster.

In common with many large cities, Sheffield's road transport system has deteriorated markedly during recent years, principally due to bus deregulation producing chaotic service patterns along roads which simply cannot cope with today's traffic volumes. Meadowhall station is ideally placed to relieve local traffic congestion if a frequent service is maintained from the local centres. It also provides an interchange with another development which could change the face of Sheffield's passenger transport system beyond recognition — the Sheffield Supertram. This eight-phase scheme is intended to be complete by summer 1995, with the first line due to open from the city centre out via Darnall and Carbrook to Meadowhall by winter 1993/94. Eventually the tracks will reach out to Wadsley Bridge, Malinbridge, Gleadless and Mosborough, and maintenance work will be carried out in a purpose-built depot close by Woodburn junction on the ex-MSLR Retford line. The new trackwork is impressive, being a mixture of tramway grooved line and (almost) conventional railway material. A great deal of civil engineering has been necessary, particularly in the city centre and around the Woodburn area, and many eyes are watching to see how much success the new system meets with, at a time when local passenger transport is lying very much in the doldrums.

What of the Sheffield railway scene today? A great part of the total system has disappeared for ever, with Wicker, Victoria and much of the ex-MSLR system having gone. Traffic to and from Retford now reaches Midland station (actually known simply as Sheffield) via a much-improved and rebuilt Nunnery curve, with the westward line to Victoria being reduced to a single-line branch to Stocksbridge Steelworks. Beyond here, nothing remains. Even the Retford traffic consists of little more than the hourly crossing of a pair of single-car Class 153 units at Woodhouse, a strange and lonely sight which belies a hectic past enjoyed by this stretch of line. Midland station remains reasonably busy, and the closure of the eastern access to Tinsley Yard from May 1993 has seen several freight trains diverted via the station roads on their way southwards. A St Pancras HST shuttle has been established, and the 'Master Cutler' has finally regained the Pullman service which once made the train famous. The 'Old Road', the line which bypassed Sheffield over 150 years ago, remains intact and is carrying a reasonable traffic flow. There is surely a touch of irony here, in that the line which was specifically built to avoid the town should remain whilst the ex-MSLR lines which did so much for the area have all but vanished from the map.

*Above:*
HSTs did not take up regular duties in the area until October 1981 when the northeast-southwest services were partially converted. Operation on the St Pancras services commenced one year later, and this view shows the 07.00 St Pancras-Sheffield service passing below Woodseats Road on 18 August 1990.

A. Taylor

*Right:*
A scene at Midland station on 27 July 1974, showing a 'Calder Valley' DMU departing on the 14.15 service to Manchester. The unit is still made up to three-car strength, and carries a working headcode indicator.

D. Griffiths

*Right:*
The passing of the Clean Air Acts from 1956 onwards helped to clean up the atmosphere to some extent, but the rear unit of this four-car set heading for Doncaster on 7 August 1990 appears to be recalling earlier days as the train passes through Attercliffe station.

A. Taylor

*Right:*
*Diesels at Dore: Class 45 No 45070 is held at signals whilst working in from the Hope Valley, and Class 40 No 40012 grinds up the climb with the Grimsby-Manchester empty newspaper vans on 27 May 1982.*

L. A. Nixon

*Right:*
*Long after the SDR system was virtually abandoned, the route was used for access to Tinsley marshalling yard and diesel loco depot. The view, looking north along the 'Old Road', shows Nos 20212 and 46043 heading towards the depot via Treeton Junction on 28 February 1977.*

G. W. Morrison

*Right:*
*A scene which is all too typical of present-day Great Britain, especially were railway establishments and property are concerned. The remains of Darnall shed in January 1993 present a far more offensive picture than any scene created there during BR steam days.*

S. R. Batty

*Right:*
*Victoria station was allowed to decay for many years after closure before demolition started in earnest during the summer of 1980. Even then, the job was done in a piecemeal fashion. Class 76 (as the 'EM1' locos became known) No 76014 heads eastwards through the site on 2 August 1978.*

D. Pearce

*Right:*
*Cast-iron columns support only the dereliction above No 1 platform in this view, taken on 2 August 1978. No 4 box has only a few freight trains and the DMU service to Penistone to handle by this time.*

D. Pearce

*Right:*
*Platform No 5, looking east.*
D. Pearce

*Right:*
*Another view of the station*
*in August 1978, looking*
*westwards from near Blast*
*Lane goods yard.*
D. Pearce

**82**

*A Metropolitan-Cammel
DMU passes through the
remains of platform No 3
with the 13.20 Sheffield-
Huddersfield on 2 August
1978.*

D. Pearce

*Right:*
*An early diesel scene in
Sheffield — English Electric
Type 1 Bo-Bo No D8050
passes through Heeley station
with a local freight working
on 8 June 1961.*

J. M. Smith

*Right:*
*One of those rare shots which
shows that diesel traction was
not always mechanically
perfect. With excessive
leakage from the train heating
system, 'Peak' No D151
departs from Midland station
with the 12.3pm to
St Pancras on 21 December
1963. Class B1 No 61152
appears to be at peace with
the world!*

D. Ian Wood

*Right:*
*Class 46 No 154 climbs away from Sheffield with a Newcastle-Bristol express on 29 May 1971. The two tracks in the foreground, recently abandoned at the time the photograph was taken, formerly carried all Hope Valley traffic.*
P. J. Rose

*Right:*
*Split-headcode English Electric Class 40 No 40134 waits for departure time with the Harwich (Parkestone Quay)-Manchester (Piccadilly) boat train on 16 August 1974. When this photograph was taken, it would have been hard to believe that in the 1990s the same train would be formed by a two-car Class 158 DMU!*
J. H. Turner

*Right:*
*Class 40 locomotives were not especially common at Sheffield, but the photographer has caught a pair in this scene. No 40038 is waiting to take forward an arrival from Poole, and No 40084 will depart on a Paignton-Leeds train. The date is 9 September 1978.*
A. R. Kaye

*Right:*
*The 'Peak' Classes 45 and 46 were associated with Sheffield throughout their working lives, seeing regular use on the Midland and northeast-southwest main lines. Class 46 No 46035 departs from Midland station with the 11.39 Poole-Newcastle train on 15 April 1978.*

G. S. Cutts

*Right:*
*The trials and tribulations of operating a fleet of worn-out DMUs led to many a cancellation, but rescue came to the salvation of passengers on the failed 16.42 Sheffield-Leeds service on 17 December 1987 in the form of pioneer Class 47 No 47401 North Eastern. The skeletal building in the rear in Sheaf House, the local BR offices.*

J. Wheeler

*Below:*
*Class 25 No 25299 and Class 40 No 40097 lift a Broughton Lane-Trafford BOC company train out of Midland station on 26 January 1983.*

L. A. Nixon

*Right:*
*The lady pedestrian appears to be feeling the full effect of a 16-cylinder exhaust as she walks above Class 40 No 40118 hauling the Cleethorpes-Manchester parcels vans past Totley Tunnel East box on 26 April 1984.*

A. Taylor

*Right:*
*Class 37s Nos 37683 and 37687 climb through Attercliffe with a Peak Forest-Selby (Melmerby Estates) stone train on 11 August 1990.*

A. Taylor

*Right:*
*Class 47 No 47117 rounds the curve at Dore & Totley with the Manchester-Harwich train on 26 August 1976. Since being diverted via the Hope Valley route, all such traffic has to reverse in Midland station. Trains are occasionally diverted via the 'Old Road' and Nunnery curve, but this is not a regular practice.*

B. Watkins

*Right:*
*The layout has been greatly altered at Dore & Totley in recent times. Only one platform survives, and a single line accommodates all traffic on the Manchester line; no platform facilities exist on the Chesterfield line, shown here occupied by a London-bound HST on a gloomy 27 January 1993.*
S. R. Batty

*Right:*
*Tinsley diesel depot services a fleet of locomotives which range far and wide in their duties. This scene of 1 May 1977 shows a collection of Classes 20 and 56, with a solitary Class 47 being serviced within the depot maintenance building. The new Class 56 locos were undergoing a thorough examination after being delivered from their Romanian builders.*
F. R. Kerr

*Right:*
*A peaceful scene at Tinsley on the afternoon of 14 February 1982. By this time the yard's busiest years were over, and decline set in rapidly from the mid-1980s.*
J. C. Hillmer

*Right:*
*Despite being built for freight purposes, Tinsley frequently hosted many locomotives regularly employed on passenger duties. 'Peak' Class 45 No 45004* Royal Irish Fusilier *takes refuge at the depot on 12 July 1981.*
                    M. J. Collins

*Right:*
*Tinsley's fleet of shunters have always been used to perform duties in Sheffield's local yards and sidings. Class 08 No 08678 leaves Rotherwood Yard for the depot on 10 February 1981.*
                    J. Fozard

*Right:*
*Class 37 No 37194 pauses at signals near Masboro' South Junction with a southbound van train on 24 July 1975.*
                    P. D. Hawkins

*Right:*
*The brightly-painted white, yellow and blue DMUs are now a long-past memory of the railway scene. A refurbished two-car set passes Holmes with a Sheffield-bound train on 28 February 1977.*
G. W. Morrison

*Below right:*
*Masborough station had plenty of platform space and always presented a neat and tidy appearance, but its location well away from the town centre was not in its favour. Perhaps the routeing of the line was chosen to favour the inhabitants of 1830s Rotherham who feared an invasion of the 'drunken and dissolute' portion of the Sheffield population! Class 40 No 40012 passes the station with a Doncaster-Sheffield ECS working on 10 September 1981.*
C. J. Marsden

*Below:.*
*The 16.06 York-Cardiff HST, diverted via the 'Old Road' due to engineering works at Nunnery Junction, passes through Rotherham on 2 June 1984.*
A. Taylor

*Right:*
*Holmes Junction on 11 May 1993, with Class 31 No 31563 heading towards Sheffield on a steel train. A withdrawn Class 47 loco can be seen below the bridge under the 'Old Road', at Booth's scrapyard, and the Rotherham Chord line lies to the extreme right.*
S. R. Batty

*Right:*
*Definitely the last train through Killamarsh GC station! Class 20 locos Nos 20021 and 20208 lift the trackwork on 17 February 1983, leaving the demolition contractors to remove the last traces. During August 1982 a new connection was brought into use at Staveley, allowing trains to run direct from Arkwright Colliery to Barrow Hill without travelling via Woodhouse Junction, where reversal was required.*
J. Wright

*Right:*
*Seen through the old goods shed at Broughton Lane on 14 September 1985, a Class 47 locomotive backs out the BOC tank train ready for departure to Manchester.*
A. Taylor

*Right:*
*The ex-GCR lines between Sheffield, Woodhouse and Rotherham have always been useful for diversions when engineering works have occupied the former MR lines. Class 47 No 47551 runs alongside the canal near Broughton Lane with the diverted 08.18 Birmingham-Leeds on 1 May 1989.*
A. Taylor

*Previous page bottom:*
*The site of the original Rotherham Central station was allowed to fall into decay after the last goods facilities were withdrawn in 1968. Resurrection came in 1987 when a brand-new establishment opened on the site on 11 May, finally giving the town a much-needed regular service between Sheffield and Doncaster. Class 08 shunter No 08436 returns with a brake van from Parkgate steelworks to Tinsley on the day after the station opened.*
L. A. Nixon

*Right:*
*'Super Sprinter' No 156481 pauses within the cramped confines of the new station with a Doncaster-Sheffield local train on 19 March 1993.*
S. R. Batty

*Right:*
*Unit No 156481 is seen returning to Doncaster a little later on the same day, whilst traversing the new 'Chord' trackwork. The ex-GCR line can be seen in the background, and train will join the line at a point between Central station and the former Ickles sidings.*
S. R. Batty

*Right:*
Class 31 No 31307 leaves Tinsley yard and joins the 'Old Road' at Treeton Junction with an up train of steel coils on 7 April 1982, during the last few weeks of semaphore-signal operation. A string of wagons can be seen in the background on the north-facing exit from the east of the yard — both these spurs were closed in May 1993.

A. Taylor

*Below:*
A last view of the 'Old Road' showing Class 31 No 31109 hauling a northbound ballast train near Canklow on 26 August 1977. The former loco shed can be seen in the right background.

L. A. Nixon

*Right:*
*A pair of Class 153 units pass at Woodburn Junction on 21 April 1993. The erstwhile signalbox has been replaced by two Portakabins, of which the left-hand one is placed on the trackbed of the former branch leading to Nunnery and City goods depots. The two lines to the right join together just out of the scene and form a single-line connection to Attercliffe Junction; the right-hand track beyond the bridge forms a single-line branch through the site of Victoria station and on to Stocksbridge steelworks.*

S. R. Batty

*Right:*
*Meadowhall station opened on 5 September 1990 to serve the retail shopping centre which transformed the adjacent derelict area. Construction work is well under way in this scene as Class 47 No 47841 passes through with the 10.15 York-Birmingham service on 17 March 1990.*

A. Taylor

*Right:*
*Class 47 No 47833 hauls the 15.22 Leeds-Sheffield train through the site on 31 March 1990. The Barnsley lines are in the foreground, and work has begun on clearing a platform space.*

A. Taylor

*Right*
*The same view three years later, showing the completed station.*

S. R. Batty

*Right*
*A Class 142 DMU leaves Meadowhall for Barnsley on 19 March 1993.*

S. R. Batty

*Below:*
*The first section of the Supertram network will be opened during winter 1993/94, when the route from the city centre to Meadowhall via Nunnery, Attercliffe and Tinsley is brought into use. This view at Meadowhall shows the Supertram tracks under construction on 19 March 1993, with the overhead equipment partly erected.*

S. R. Batty

*Right:*
*The former Tinsley South Junction in March 1993. In the foreground is the singled ex-GCR route leading from Broughton Lane to Tinsley East, and the former connection through to Tinsley West and Barnsley can be seen to have been replaced by Supertram trackwork.*

S. R. Batty

*Right:*
*Supertrams will approach Meadowhall along the former GCR Barnsley line before turning left and climbing steeply into the platforms. The original line passed below the MR by means of the underbridge shown here.*

S. R. Batty

*Right:*
*The Supertram depot at Nunnery in April 1993.*

S. R. Batty

*Single-car Class 153 unit No 153326 leaves Woodhouse and heads for Retford on 19 March 1993. This once-hectic railway location is now virtually devoid of railway activity, apart from the hourly passage of these units.*